An Eliza Book

Elizabeth K. Fischer

Monarch Tree
PUBLISHING

Eau Claire, Wisconsin

Published by Monarch Tree Publishing, 3922 26th Street,
Elk Mound, Wisconsin 54739.
First printing November, 2023.

ISBN   978-1-7331087-9-9

Library of Congress Control Number: 2023918385

Cover Design: Shawna Lou Creative
Layout: Elizabeth Fischer

Dedicated to Scott o' the Trees

who helped me so much

after two tragedies in my life

and

struggled with red vibrations.

Acknowledgments

Thank you, Shawna Lou Stanley, for your artistic talent, accurate interpretation, and authentic tweaks to the presentation of *Mittka*.

Books by Elizabeth K. Fischer

The Eliza Series

Trouble at the North Pole

The Last Christmas Tree

The Trapped Wizard

Teeny Tiny Elf's Mistake

Riding the Rainbow

The Healing Touch

The Face of Treachery

The Disturbance

Mittka

All of Elizabeth's books may be ordered in print and are available in for rental in audio at monarchtreepublishing.com.

Business and Marketing Books

Mistakes I Made My First Five Years in Business

What's in It for Me? Marketing from the Customer's Point of View

Mistakes I Made Buying Advertising

Chapter 1

"Santa! Mrs. Claus! Wake up!" was urgently whispered in their ears.

"Santa! Mrs. Claus! Wake up!" was repeated until the room reverberated with the intense request.

Both came out of Dreamland simultaneously. Having their attention, the sylph leader declared, "The Disturbance has been detected in the deep ocean. The water babies are tracking it. We're off to follow in the air. We'll be back when we know more."

With that, the roomful of sylphs vanished.

They heard a knock on their door. "Come in," Santa commanded.

Navva rushed into the room, breathless. "The sylphs

just woke me. The Disturbance is back. Do you think she's in it?"

Before they could answer, the sylphs reappeared. In a very tense tone, they uttered, "The structure broke apart. We're searching for survivors. We'll bring them to the South and Indian Ocean Dome. Meet us there."

"I'll let Teeny Tiny Elf know," Mrs. Claus mumbled as she swung out of bed.

Santa, Mrs. Claus, and Navva's constant vigilance and worry over the last nine days skyrocketed to a new height. The three quickly dressed and hurriedly transported to the Dome, not even considering breakfast. When they arrived, they were surprised to note the dark sky. "I was so excited about the sylphs message that I didn't register the time of day," noted Navva.

Those in the structure heard it groaning and felt its shaking increase. Rising from her comfortable seat, Eliza addressed Lugh, Brennan, Cade, and Eanna who were closer to the entrance. "Don your energy exchangers. Be ready to exit. I think the structure is coming apart." Giving each of the crew a hug and Lugh a hug and a kiss, she urged, "Don't worry about Sarah and me. Get out. I have a strong premonition the sylphs have been searching for me and are on top of this. I suspect they will have a rescue team at the ready."

"Where are you headed?" Lugh asked.

"To the control area," Eliza responded. "I want to outfit Anax, Doolin, the AIs, and the instrument panels in energy exchangers."

"See you on the beach," Lugh finished, mustering a brave smile.

"Be certain all of you make it," Eliza added. "I don't want to face Fiona if you don't."

Hoping this was not good-bye, Lugh echoed, "We will. You be sure to make it, too. I don't want to face your parents and Navva if you don't."

With one last look at Lugh and the crew, Eliza hurried down the hall. "C'mon, Sarah, let's check out control."

Anax, Doolin, and the AIs were so disoriented from being thrown around the area when the structure swerved that they didn't notice Eliza enter. *Sarah, before I don my energy exchanger huddle near me like you did when we dove into the water. I'm surrounding your essence along with my body.*

Okay.

She had barely released the thought when the structure started to shake violently. She crowded close to Eliza who covered Anax, each AI, Doolin, the two instrument panels, and herself separately with energy exchangers. The structure emitted a last groan and fell apart. Those in the control room were ejected out that end while Lugh and the crew were expelled out the other.

The deep ocean water babies discovered Lugh and his crew first. *Grab onto one of us,* they directed. *We'll take you to the water babies higher up who will get you to the dragons.*

Four dragons who had been nearby settled onto the water just as the shallow water babies surfaced with Lugh and his crew. *Climb aboard and hang on,* the lead dragon instructed. *We're flying part way and will finish in the water to bring you onto the beach at the dome.*

The leprechauns had an exhilarating flight, mostly with their eyes closed. When they plunged back down to the water, Cade and Brennan felt ready to pass out. They didn't. Once they were moving through the water, all four had the sense of being home. Surfacing one at a time, each dragon dropped off its passenger and dove down into the water again.

Lugh was the first to slosh through the shallows onto the beach. De-materializing his energy exchanger, he briskly stood up straight, glad to be back. Santa wrapped him in a big hug. "Welcome back, my friend! We are thrilled to see you!"

As Santa moved on to welcome Cade, Brennan, and Eanna, Mrs. Claus gave Lugh a kiss on the cheek and hugged him tightly. "Lugh! Lugh! We were afraid we had lost you!"

"Not with your daughter around. She is really something," he replied, swiveling around to catch Eliza's eye. He didn't see her.

Mrs. Claus gasped. "She isn't here. Is she with you?"

"She was…"

Those from the control room were having difficulty. They had been tossed amid an underwater rock formation. The AIs were struggling to throw off their energy exchangers. Eliza caught the attention of two deep ocean water babies. *Each of you grab one of them and hold it toward me, please.*

They promptly did what she had requested. Looking from one to the other, Eliza mentally commanded them, *Be still. We will get you back to dry ground. Do exactly what you are told by each being who will give you a ride.*

Sarah mentally praised, *Good job, Eliza. Those are just the instructions they will heed. You might be a tech person yet.*

Eliza chuckled. *Take them. Be sure whoever is handling them receives these instructions. Thank you.*

The deep ocean water babies followed Eliza's directions completely. When the shallow water babies were passing the AIs along to the dragons, the sylphs overheard. The lead one rushed to the dome. Thankfully Tech Elf and Shorty had arrived. The sylph singled them out and related the commands just as they had been told to the dragons. "Sounds like AIs," volunteered Shorty.

Tech Elf agreed. "Santa, we need help with the next two. They are AIs and aren't good in the water."

"We'll help with one," offered Lugh.

As the dragons surfaced, Lugh and his crew pulled off one AI, and Santa and Navva grabbed the other, not releasing them until they were on dry sand.

Eliza had lost track of Anax. *Sarah, did you see where Anax went? Is he swimming?*

No, I caught sight of him floating. I wonder if he was knocked unconscious?

Where is he?

I think he's behind that tall rock with the pointed top.

Eliza circled around to the other side of the formation. She came up beside him. He had caught his energy exchanger on a jagged piece of rock, tearing it open and sticking to the rock. Eliza stretched for him, unhooking him from the rock with her left hand and sealing the tear with her right.

Doolin was nearby, appearing frightened. To calm him, she projected an image and emotion of safety. *Breathe*

6

normally, she instructed. *The energy exchanger I put on you is protecting you in the water. A water baby will get you to the surface, and we'll get to dry land from there. I'll be right behind you and bring Anax.*

Addressing the deep ocean water babies surrounding her, Eliza asked, *Would you please gather all the pieces of the structure you can find along with the instrument panels and give them to the shallow water babies to get to the South and Indian Ocean Dome? I want them at the North Pole so that we can reconstruct it.*

They readily agreed.

Eliza looked at the deep ocean water baby beside Doolin. *Please guide Doolin and me to the surface.*

As she began to move, pulling Anax along with her, another deep ocean water baby flanked his other side, easing Eliza's effort by helping to drag him. Together, they hauled him higher to the shallow water babies. Before leaving, Eliza extended her gratitude to the deep ocean ones. *Thank you and your fellow deep ocean water babies for your help. We are very grateful.*

She thought she detected a smile. *You are most welcome. We are not accustomed to being appreciated,* he replied.

Several shallow water babies escorted Eliza to the surface where Eva, Len, Merna, and a huge gathering of sylphs waited. "Eliza!" they screamed in unison.

She smiled broadly. "I am glad to see you, my friends! Thanks for your help. I knew I could rely on you."

I don't mean to be annoying, but I'm getting claustrophobic. Could you have your reunion in the dome once we are back? Sarah whispered.

"I have Sarah tucked into my energy exchanger, and she is getting antsy to be home. See you there. Thanks, water babies, for all your help. We are extremely grateful."

She turned to Doolin. Sweeping her hand to indicate Merna, Len, and Eva, Eliza explained, *I know you are out of your comfort zone here and have never ridden on a dragon's back. Do you want to try or would you like to be carried in a dragon's mouth?*

His eyes widened. Both prospects generated fear in him.

Would you like me to make you sleep during the ride? She offered.

He quickly assented. Eliza applied a light freeze on him, prompting him to become unaware of what he was about to experience.

Swimming over to Merna with Doolin and Anax in tow, she asked, "Would you and Len carry Anax and Doolin in your mouths? Anax is unconscious already, and I put a light freeze on Doolin. I'm adding a little to Anax just to be certain he doesn't come to and freak out in your mouth." She smirked at Eva. "I'll catch a ride on Eva."

Merna carefully accepted Anax, and Len gently wrapped his jaws around Doolin. When she was certain both were securely in place, Eliza swam over and climbed aboard Eva. "Thank you, shallow water babies! Let's go!"

Waving to the water babies as the dragons climbed into the sky, Eliza thrilled to the smooth ride provided by Eva's massive wings. When Eva nosedived back to the water, Eliza enjoyed every bit of the journey. As the three surfaced in the dome, Merna opened her mouth wide. Santa and Navva retrieved Anax who was just coming out of his freeze. Cade and Brennan pulled Doolin out of Len's mouth.

Eliza slid off Eva and gave her, Merna, and Len each a hug. "I asked the deep ocean water babies to collect as much of the structure and the instrument panels as they could find. Would you get those items and bring them here, please?"

She noticed Tech Elf and Shorty. "Hi, guys! Len, Merna, and Eva will bring the pieces of the structure and the instrument panels back here. Would you transport those to a place where you can reconstruct the structure?"

Giving her a big hug, Tech Elf expressed, "We have been terrified about you. Where have you been?"

Pulling away from Tech Elf, she stooped to give Shorty a hug, too. "I'm sure Dad will want to know the entire story. After you have all the pieces, join us in the kitchen."

She mentally heard the sound of a throat being cleared. *Sarah! Oh, Sarah, I am so sorry to keep you.*

Opening the energy exchanger, Sarah zipped out. She sighed with pleasure. *Ahhh. I have a new appreciation for freedom!*

Out loud, Eliza added, "Here's Sarah, too. I was so thankful to have her along."

By that time Eliza's parents and Navva were standing behind her. She gave her mother a big hug and a kiss on the cheek. "Mother, I am happy to see you in the flesh! I am sorry you witnessed my being swallowed by the Disturbance. Are you okay?"

Mrs. Claus hugged her daughter tightly. "I am now that you have returned. I feared you were not able to come back." Pulling away, she looked quizzically at Eliza. "What do you mean, 'in the flesh'?"

"I'll tell you later," Eliza replied, giving her mother another tight hug and a kiss on the cheek.

She turned to her dad and wrapped her arms around him. "Thank you, Dad, for your wise advice and excellent training!"

Returning her hug, Santa, too, was perplexed. What did that statement mean?

Before Santa could ask, Navva plucked her into his arms. "You're back! I am so relieved. I thought you were gone for good." He gripped her tightly and didn't want to let go.

Finally, she was able to disengage enough to give him a loving kiss which seemed to calm him. Her eyes sparkled. "I missed you, too. I love you, Navva," she murmured, followed by one more loving kiss.

Santa glanced down and noticed Doolin coming out of his freeze. Santa's brow furrowed. "What are you doing on the ground, Lugh? Were you hurt?"

Doolin gave Santa a blank stare. Eliza was reading her dad's thoughts as he quizzically reviewed Lugh/Doolin's actions. She didn't know how long she could handle this, but submerging her thoughts about Doolin as Santa had taught her to do regarding Navva, she offered, "What's the matter, Dad?"

He gave her a perplexed stare but couldn't read her mind. Why is she blocking me about Lugh? He thought. "When Lugh came out of the water, I gave him a big hug. Now he's on the ground. He has his energy exchanger back on. What's wrong? Has he been sick?"

Barely holding back her chuckles, Eliza managed to assume a straight face and mirrored his concern. "He was fine in the structure."

Kneeling down next to Doolin, Santa dissipated the energy exchanger and placed his hand on Doolin's forehead. Doolin leaped up in alarm, quickly backing quite a distance away from Santa.

Cade, Brennan, and Eanna were behind Santa, doing their best to restrain their laughter. Lugh was nowhere to be seen. As the guys had planned, Lugh had ducked behind a large plant out of sight. Making him jump, Teeny Tiny Elf walked up beside Lugh and wondered, "Why are you hiding by this plant, Lugh?"

That broke the floodgates of laughter. The crew rolled on the ground, and even Eliza had to sit down on the beach, doubled over.

Santa looked from Doolin to Lugh who was also on the ground, laughing. "What?!"

"Welcome to a taste of what we've been through, Dad," Eliza eked out between bouts of laughter.

Teeny Tiny Elf goblin moved into Eliza's lap. "You're back! And you're okay! What a happy day!" He spotted Doolin. "Why are there two Lughs?"

"Good question," Santa responded. Realizing his daughter, good friend, and the crew were behind their laughter, Santa stepped over to Eliza, pulled her up along with Teeny Tiny Elf, and gave her a bear hug. "You will pay for this," he whispered into her ear.

"Eliza's in trouble. I'm outta here," Teeny Tiny Elf announced, jumping into Mrs. Claus's arms.

As he exited, Santa finished his statement to Eliza. "I have missed you so much and couldn't stop worrying about where you were and if you were alright."

She kissed him on the cheek, pressed her cheek lovingly against his, and whispered back, "I know. Your reaction was worth every bit of the retribution you will dole out. I love you, Dad."

By that time, Mrs. Claus and Navva had grasped the situation and were also chuckling. "You got your father well, Dear. I have never seen him so baffled."

"Not only did I experience his physical reaction, I also read his mind," Eliza shared. "When he realized what we had done, he rapidly perused a list of what to do to me." She lapsed back into laughter.

More than ever before, Navva comprehended Santa and Eliza's unique relationship, which was beyond father-daughter, mentor-protégé, or wizard par excellence-trainee. They were kindred spirits who shared similar personalities. For the first time he questioned if he could fit into this family.

Chapter 2

Eliza motioned to Doolin. *I'm sorry Dad alarmed you. He and Lugh are life-long friends. He thought you were Lugh and was worried. We set him up to mistake you for Lugh because Dad is a jokester and pulling a good joke on him is not easy. Please step beside me so that I can introduce you.*

Doolin did. With her arm still wrapped around Santa, Eliza presented, "Dad, this is Doolin. He and Lugh look remarkably identical. He had caught glimpses of Lugh's life, which is what instigated the Disturbance." She turned to Doolin. "Doolin this is Santa."

"Santa!? The great wizard Santa!?" Eliza thought Doolin might faint. Instead, he bowed. "I am honored, Sir."

14

"Thank you. I apologize for my daughter's delayed introduction." He smirked at her. "She can get caught up in having fun."

Eliza noticed that Anax was coming out of his freeze. Keeping her arm around her dad, Eliza brought him with her to check on Anax. Dissipating Anax's energy exchanger, she telepathically relayed to Santa, *I have already alarmed you once today. I won't do it twice. Anax has a ring of eyes around his head. He can open one, all nine, or any number between at once. He communicates in images and emotion. He seemed to be unconscious after we ejected from the structure. Would you take a look at him, please?*

As she removed her arm, Santa smiled into her eyes. "I love you, too, Daughter, and will gladly do that."

Santa hunkered down beside Anax, projecting as he did, *I'm Santa, Eliza's father. She tells me that you became unconscious when you left the structure. How do you feel?*

Dizzy.

Did you hit your head when the structure fell apart?

Anax hesitated. *Maybe. I don't remember what happened.*

I don't think you ought to walk right now. Are you okay with my picking you up? I'll take you to my home where you can rest, Santa explained.

That's okay. I feel tired, Anax finished. He closed his eyes.

Gently sliding his arms underneath Anax, Santa transported the two of them to Eliza's bedroom and placed Anax on the bed.

Mrs. Claus looked around. "Let's transport to the kitchen," she suggested. "I'll make breakfast, and you five can tell us what happened. We are all anxious to know."

"Mrs. Claus's food!" Cade exclaimed. "What a reward for making it back!"

Eliza stepped over to Navva, slid her hand into his, and smiled. "Ahhh…the comforts of home. Seeing everyone I love, being near you, and savoring Mom's cooking." She kissed him on the cheek and leaned her head on his shoulder.

Leaving Tech Elf and Shorty to process the pieces from the structure and handle the AIs, Mrs. Claus transported Eliza, Navva, Doolin, Lugh, Cade, Brennan, Eanna, and Teeny Tiny Elf to the kitchen. Santa was just entering as they arrived. "I'm guessing he has a concussion, but being unfamiliar with his physical form, I'm not certain. I asked my body elemental to speak with his for more information," Santa divulged. "Take a seat, everyone. Before you begin, Eliza, I'm contacting Merlin to join us."

Dusty and Chance ran up to Eliza. "Hi, babies!" She

hunkered down, hugged them both, and looked up at Navva. "Thanks for taking care of them."

"They've been sleeping in your bedroom with me."

Nuzzling noses first with Dusty and then Chance, Eliza noted, "That's where you like to sleep, isn't it, guys?"

Mrs. Claus whispered in Lugh's ear. "What does Doolin like to eat?"

"We have no idea," he murmured. "We did not see him eat nor did he offer us food."

She was taken aback. "Really?"

Lugh smiled. "Eliza materialized all the food we ate."

"That's too bad," Mrs. Claus replied sympathetically.

"Serve him what you serve us. We'll find out what he takes in, if he does, by testing him," Lugh suggested.

Navva and Eliza settled into seats between Lugh and Santa. She addressed Cade, Brennan, and Eanna. "Do you want to go home today or would you like to stay here for a day, rest, and clean up before you go home?" She glanced at her mother. "I'm sure Mother would serve you several delicious meals to help you catch up."

"That's a good idea, Dear," Mrs. Claus concurred. "Stay until tomorrow, guys. You'll get rested, refreshed, and full before you leave." She grinned at her daughter. "While I'm sure she did her best, living off Eliza's materialized food has not been tasty."

"To her credit, she warned us of that," Lugh noted. "We were glad for something, anything to eat."

"Yes," echoed Eanna. "We were thankful you taught her materializing, Santa."

"After we eat, let's contact our families and let them know we are back and safe," Cade suggested. "Once they are aware we're home, I'm sure they won't mind our staying until tomorrow."

"Good idea," Brennan agreed.

Lugh turned to Santa. "I hear your visit to Fiona was fun."

Santa chuckled. "Oh, yes, Fiona was fun alright, especially when she didn't know your whereabouts. Mrs. Claus and Eliza helped me that day."

"I recommend you contact her before Cade, Brennan, and Eanna reach their families. She will not be happy hearing from someone else that you have returned," Mrs. Claus remarked.

Remembering their visit, Eliza agreed. "For Dad's sake, make certain she is first."

Lugh smirked at his good friend. "Will that make up for today?"

"Today?!" Santa returned. "What about our visit to her that you arranged and missed?"

Mrs. Claus broke into a hearty laugh. "Today Santa was baffled. He probably will not appreciate this characterization, but that day he was cowed."

"I know I'm already in trouble," Eliza added, joining her mother's laughter, "but cowed is an apt description of Dad that day. I was amazed."

Before Santa could defend himself, Merlin materialized, immediately walking over to Eliza, pulling her up, and giving her a big hug. "All of us, including me, were scared. I am elated you have returned and are healthy." Turning and keeping one arm around Eliza, he addressed Lugh and the crew. "That applies to you, too, Lugh, Cade, Brennan, and Eanna. Seeing all of you safe is a wonderful way to start the day!"

Sarah injected, *How about me?*

Merlin acknowledged her. *Sorry, Sarah, we were shocked when you were missing and are very thankful you were with them. How did that happen?*

Sarah's answer was delayed by the appearance of Tech Elf and Shorty. "We have all the pieces and the instrument panels the water babies could find," Tech Elf reported. "Why do you want them?"

"Sit," Eliza directed both. "You will understand once we finish." She paused, returning her attention to Sarah. "Sarah, would you please answer Merlin's question?"

I had had an uneasy feeling about Eliza the day she was swallowed by the Disturbance so I stayed close to her. When she got sucked in, I did, too.

"As she filled my mind with comments, I realized she was with me and asked her to contact Dad or leave for help. She had already tried both with no success," Eliza related. She addressed Santa. "I didn't know that spiritual energy could be trapped."

"Neither did we," Merlin returned before Santa could answer.

Glancing around at Lugh, Cade, Brennan, and Eanna, Eliza continued, "The five of us and Sarah, too, now know how, don't we?"

In response to their nods, Eliza launched into telling what had happened to them. With insertions here and there from the guys and Sarah, their eating breakfast was finished long before they completed their story. Eliza, Lugh, Santa, and Mrs. Claus had noticed that Doolin did not imbibe the essence of the food as the other leprechauns had done.

Eliza singled out Doolin. "We have not asked you what you take in for nourishment. I see you didn't touch your food as Lugh, Cade, Brennan, and Eanna did. Are you alright? Aren't you hungry?"

"We don't have food. We have water."

"Are you telling me…" Eliza stopped, caught up in her epiphany. She had been told by the water babies on Nona that small life lived in the water. She assumed they had meant amoebas or plankton. With the loss of available plant and animal life, the Nona beings had adapted to surviving on those microscopic creatures. No wonder they needed better access to water! It was their only sustenance, not just the liquid but also the creatures living inside. Eliza comprehended better than ever Nona beings' desperate straits.

She shared the revelation with everyone.

Mrs. Claus telepathically contacted Parv, the Royal Elf in charge of the South and Indian Ocean Dome, asking him to bring a gallon of water containing plankton to her kitchen immediately. He appeared a couple minutes later. "Thank you, Parv."

"Why do you want it?" he wondered.

"On the planet where our visitors reside, all the plant and animal life has died. The only remaining life is microscopic organisms in the water. They need this for nourishment," Mrs. Claus replied.

"Wow! I'm glad we have this for them. Let me know when you need more," Parv suggested before transporting back to the dome.

She poured some into a glass and brought it to Doolin. "Try this," she encouraged.

He did, quickly absorbing the entire amount. "Would you like more?" Mrs. Claus offered. "I want you to have enough but not too much."

"I think I can handle another," he returned.

As he took in the second glass, Mrs. Claus poured a small amount into another glass and handed it to Santa. "I know you are about to check on Anax. Take this with you."

Santa smiled. Mrs. Claus always anticipated his next move. Taking the glass from her, he headed for Eliza's bedroom.

Anax had regained consciousness. Holding the glass toward him, Santa communicated, *Doolin is enjoying this water, which is similar to what you have on Nona. Would you like some, too?*

Surprised at Santa's care and kindness, Anax accepted the glass and imbibed the water. When he finished, Santa asked, *Would you like more right now or would you like to rest and have more later?*

I'm still dizzy. I'll rest right now. Thank you.

Okay. I'll be back to check on you in a while, Santa replied and returned to the kitchen.

"Anax had regained consciousness. He liked it, too," Santa informed everyone.

"How do you have this?" Doolin wondered.

"We are raising fish in the water of that dome so we have a plentiful amount there," Mrs. Claus explained.

Eliza caught Doolin's attention. "I am sorry. I did not realize the reason why you needed water so badly." She turned to her dad. "Dad, we must help them. Everyone, alive or dead, on that planet is trapped by the layer of energy. We have to dissipate that layer into the ether."

"How do you propose we do that, Daughter?"

"I figured you would know."

Santa raised his eyebrows. "You did, did you?"

"Yes, you know how to handle everything."

Mrs. Claus chuckled. "This is the result of wishing for a daughter, Dear. She has complete confidence in you to address any issue, whether you think you can or not. A son would have understood that you have restraints. He would not have had such lofty expectations." She halted. "I agree with Eliza. I'm certain you can do it."

Santa sighed and looked at Merlin. "What do you think?"

"I am appreciating not having a wife and daughter."

"Santa does whatever they want," Teeny Tiny Elf inserted. "He will not rest until he fulfills Eliza's request."

Santa glared at Teeny Tiny Elf, knowing he was correct. Santa's gaze shifted to Lugh. "Did she promise this to the residents of Nona?"

"I think so."

"Why didn't you stop her?" Santa insisted.

"I was sleeping the first time she mentioned it," Lugh explained, attempting to wiggle out of any responsibility.

"Just like you, Lugh did ask me how I was going to accomplish that," Eliza defended. "He seemed very dubious when I stated you would take care of it." She looked at Tech Elf and Shorty. "In answer to your question, Tech Elf, I wanted to save the structure so that you could put it back together. I think this layer of energy must be tackled from the inside and the outside simultaneously. The only way to access the inside is via the structure."

"We have not seen material of its nature," he commented.

"The atmosphere responds to wishes. I suspect the makers asked the atmosphere to assemble what was in their minds, and this structure was the result. The atmosphere likely developed the material to suit the makers' request," Eliza described.

"That's cool!" Shorty exclaimed.

Tech Elf nodded. "I'd like that option. Think it and it appears. Wow!"

"That's what happened to me when I first dove into the water," Eliza noted. "I mumbled that I would like a light and one came on."

"How do we find this planet?" Navva questioned. "According to what you just told us, it is cloaked by the layer."

Eliza smiled at him. "That was my concern. To discover more about the outside of the layer, I asked Doolin to come back with us. Knowing how leprechauns easily move though time, I thought we could take Doolin and Lugh back to find their common ancestor. He could give us information about the location of the planet and what precipitated his clan's going there."

They heard a loud hum, and sylphs filled the room. "We'd like to go with you. We have been stumped that we could not find you after you disappeared. We'd like our curiosity satisfied by locating the planet."

"Hello, my friends," Eliza grinned. "I was certain you would join us, particularly when I mentioned this idea. We'd like you along, too."

"Well, Daughter, I'm impressed by your thinking through and taking actions to give us the opportunity to help. I agree that both outside and inside efforts must be applied, likely together. I think tracing Lugh and Doolin's common ancestor is wise. Let's start with that," Santa suggested.

"You certainly present challenging situations, Eliza," Merlin remarked. "I'm in to help. When do you want to go back in time?"

"Tech Elf," Santa began, "How long until the structure's reconstruction is complete?"

"I have no idea."

"Start on it right away. I recommend you rebuild it in the South and Indian Ocean Dome so it is near where we need to launch it."

Tech Elf nodded. "Shorty, Sarah, and I left the materials there with just that thought."

"Gather as many elves as you need to help," Santa continued. "Getting it finished is a high priority."

"In answer to your question, Merlin, let's go this afternoon. These beings require all the help we can give them as soon as we can do that. Let's not delay. Eliza is right; we need more information and a visit to the exterior of the planet before we can decide how to proceed."

Eliza pulled Doolin into the discussion. "Are you okay with going back in time with us today, Doolin?"

"I don't know how," he replied.

"Santa will lead us," Lugh assured him, glancing at his good friend. "This will be very interesting."

"Contact Fiona right now," emphasized Mrs. Claus. "Take care of your talk with her. Then Eanna, Cade, and Brennan, reach your families."

"Once we have that done, could we help you rebuild the structure, Tech Elf?" Brennan wondered.

"Absolutely! We would love to have your expertise," Tech Elf enthused.

Great! Your help frees up Tech Elf, Shorty, and me to work on the instrument panels and AIs, Sarah remarked.

Chapter 3

Lugh moved to the living room for privacy contacting Fiona. *We're back!* He announced.

Lugh! Where were you? I have been worried sick about you.

Beings from another planet wanted an apparatus like we have in the ocean domes so that they could get better access to water. They grabbed us to build it.

Why didn't they just ask for help?

They didn't know how and were desperate.

I heard that Eliza had been snatched by the Disturbance. Was she with you?

Yes, we are all back safe and sound.

She sighed. *Good! When are you coming over? I want to discuss when I move in. I'm keeping a closer eye on you.*

Lugh paused, stunned. *Well, some leprechauns live on that planet, too-*

Leprechauns on another planet?!

Yeah, in fact the one we have met, Doolin, looks just like me.

Really?! I want to meet him!

We fooled Santa into thinking Doolin was me.

You did?! I want to hear more.

I'll give you the whole episode later. The residents of the planet have a big problem. A layer of energy surrounding the planet is holding back spiritual energy, restraining it from dissipating into the ether. We are going on a time travel today to find my common ancestor with Doolin, in hopes of locating the planet.

Wait a minute… Fiona paused, thinking. *I vaguely remember hearing a story about your clan and another planet.* She hesitated. *Who was involved in that? Fitz…Fitzsimmons. Do you have an ancestor Fitzsimmons?*

Yeah, he's my great-grandfather.

I think that story came from him. Try him.

We will. Thanks. I'll let you know when we are back and how he worked out.

Be careful, Lugh.

I will. I love you, Fiona.

I love you, too, Lugh.

Walking back into the kitchen, Lugh encountered Santa and Mrs. Claus returning from Anax. "I introduced Mrs.

29

Claus to Anax so she could check on him while we are gone," Santa explained.

She turned to Teeny Tiny Elf. "Would you please stay here and help me? I would appreciate having you here."

"Okay. What do you want me to do?" he wondered.

"Help me keep tabs on Anax and what is happening with the rebuilding at the dome."

"I can do both!"

Lugh looked from Santa to Eliza. "Fiona suggested we go back to my great-grandfather Fitzsimmons. She thought she had heard about part of my clan going to another planet and traced it back to him."

"That's a big help!" exclaimed Eliza. "If she is right, we will move forward quickly."

"Who is going?" Santa asked, pointing at each as he continued, "Merlin, Eliza, Navva, Lugh, Doolin, and me, right?"

They all nodded agreement, including Doolin.

"We're transporting to the South and Indian Ocean Dome where we will contact our families and then help reconstruct the structure," Eanna noted.

"We'll see you when you get back," Brennan added.

"Yeah," Cade remarked, "we'll be interested to hear what you learn."

Stepping next to them, Tech Elf effused, "Sarah, Shorty, and I will go with you. We appreciate your help!"

As they disappeared, Santa directed the rest, "Gather near me. Lugh, think of your great-grandfather. I'll trace him through time and take us to his location."

They materialized next to a traditional cottage in Ireland. Tap! Tap! Tap! Someone was busy. Following the sound of continuous tapping, they walked through a propped-open door and halted in shock. Sunlight was streaming in a window onto a leprechaun putting the finishing touch on a pair of shoes. He looked up at the visitors and was stunned.

He was a third Lugh! The first to find his voice, he stated the obvious. "I can tell by yer faces that ye must be kin. Yer strange garb means ye aren't from around these parts. Who are ye?"

His wife opened a door leading into the residence. "Who are ye speaking to, Fitzsimmons?"

Noticing the visitors, her jaw dropped. Two of them were carbon copies of her husband! Regaining her composure, she invited, "Come in and take a seat. Fitzsimmons, stop for a bit. Would ye like some tea?"

As she held the door, Santa, Merlin, Eliza, Navva, Lugh, and Doolin followed her directions. "We would appreciate some tea," Lugh replied, not registering Doolin's situation. He addressed his great-grandfather. "I am your great-grandson Lugh." Pointing to each as he introduced, he continued, "Beside me is my good friend Santa, his daughter Eliza, her friend Navva, and Merlin. Since he is the spit'n image of you and me, Doolin seems to be a relative, but we don't know more."

"We are pleased to meet ye, Grandson," Fitzsimmons's wife expressed. "I am Sadhbh, yer great-grandmother."

"Merlin?! Santa?!" Fitzsimmons blurted. "Ye associate with wizards?"

"Yes, he does," Santa answered. "We have been good friends for many years. I am pleased to meet you both."

Fitzsimmons eyed Lugh. "Ye certainly have raised the status of our family, rubbin' elbows with Merlin, Santa, and his family. My goodness!"

He looked at Doolin. "I know who ye are. Ye are the grandson of my twin brother Feidhelm." Shaking his head, he added, "I told him another planet was not the answer to his wanderin'. Said he trusted Nona more than humans. Humph! Why don't ye take in yer tea?"

"He can't," Lugh responded. "Our kin left alive on that planet are starving. They only imbibe water with small creatures inside."

"Is that what yer here fer?" Fitzsimmons questioned.

As Lugh nodded, Santa explained, "Most of the beings on the planet along with the plants and animals have died. Their rapid die-off precipitated a layer of energy which now surrounds the planet, trapping their spiritual energy and cloaking the planet."

"So ye can't find it?" Fitzsimmons assessed.

In unison, Lugh, Merlin, and Santa shook their heads. "Can you help us?" Santa asked.

Fitzsimmons glanced at his wife and sighed. "I 'supose I'd better help kin." Returning his attention to Santa and Lugh, he replied, "Before Feidhelm left for good he took me to visit. If we went back in time to that day, I could take ye there. Would that work?"

Eliza blurted excitedly, "Yes! That would be very helpful. Thank you!"

He eyed her. "I'll close me shop for a bit and go with ye."

When he left the room, Sadhbh touched Eliza's arm and whispered in her ear, "Thank ye for helping our kin. Fitzsimmons loves his brother and was frustrated with the move."

Upon his return, Santa offered, "We have quite a group so I'll transport, if you don't mind. Since we will be in an atmosphere that's different from normal, let's all don energy exchangers. I'll put one on you, Fitzsimmons. When you come home, just ask it to leave you, and it will."

In response to Fitsimmons's nod, Santa added, "I'll read your mind for our destination."

Suddenly they were hovering in the atmosphere above a planet, not with the appearance of the one today cloaked by the impenetrable layer of energy. This one was clear. They noticed what appeared to be land masses and water on the planet's surface. Sylphs materialized all around.

Fitzsimmons spied them. "The sylphs are helping ye, eh?" He paused. "Yer goin' need all the help ye can get." Looking at the sylphs, Merlin, Lugh, and Santa, he finished, "This is as much as I kin do." Turning to Doolin, he noted, "I hope this works out for ye."

Then Fitzsimmons disappeared back home.

"Lugh note this date," Santa requested. "Let's go forward through time and see when the layer begins to form."

"We've pinpointed the planet's location," the lead sylph volunteered. "We'll stay here in case you find anything more that will be helpful."

"Good," Santa replied.

They watched the planet change from vibrancy to

devastation. At certain points Santa had Lugh, Merlin, Eliza, or Navva remember the date. When they arrived at the current date, the planet disappeared completely from sight. Santa backed up to the last murky view they had had of the planet. He advanced slowly, noting dates, and once again they observed it vanish.

Santa turned to Merlin. "Do you want to see more before we transport back to the North Pole?"

In response to Merlin's perplexed look, Santa continued, "How about you Eliza, Navva, Lugh, Doolin, sylphs? Can we learn more?"

"I think I know your answer, but I'm asking the question anyway," Eliza began. "Can we go back to this time and erase the problem?"

Santa shook his head. "We could affect too many unknowns."

"Would you go back again?" Merlin requested. "Move even more slowly forward. What prompted the gathering of energy? Did some particular event or being?"

They took another look but found the entire planet too much to watch. "Let's take a different approach," Santa suggested. "We'll split viewing the planet into quadrants. Eliza, take the upper left, Navva the upper right, Merlin the lower right. I'll handle the lower left. Lugh keep an eye on the left half and Doolin the right half. With that focus and those overlaps we have a better chance to catch the changes."

Returning to the murky panorama, Santa inched the scene forward while all six stared intently. Eliza noticed a big clump. Santa saw one about the same time. "Stop!" she cried. He did. "What was that?"

"I spotted a big burst of energy," Santa commented.

"See that?" Eliza pointed. "I think a second one caught onto the first."

"I detected a similar happening," Navva offered.

"I did, too," Merlin agreed.

"Keep your eyes on those areas," Santa directed, fast forwarding to the present. "Do we still see them? Lugh and Doolin, you watch, too."

Simultaneously, Lugh and Doolin both declared, "A third big eruption of energy just happened with a second right behind which attached to the first."

"So six events happened in a short period of time," Santa summarized.

Eliza thought of Evanescing. "Could we talk to those six energy clumps? That was the secret to the sylphs' success with Evanescing."

"What would we ask?" wondered Merlin.

"Discover where they came from, tell what has happened to the planet, and ask if they would be willing to move away from the planet," she suggested.

"That is an excellent idea," Santa affirmed. "Communicate with the ones in your quadrant: Eliza and I will take the left, Navva and Merlin the right, and Lugh and Doolin the center." He paused. "Don't ask them to leave just yet. If they are willing, inform them we will be back to give them the signal to do that."

They had the same challenge Eliza encountered when she spoke to the energy that had become attached to wizards, getting the energy's attention. The sylphs helped. Each team used innovative tactics to have the energy realize it was being addressed. Once they were finished, Santa directed, "Let's go home and discuss our findings."

"We're ready to return whenever you want," the sylphs volunteered and then disappeared.

Chapter 4

They arrived to an empty kitchen. Both Mrs. Claus and Teeny Tiny Elf were nowhere in sight. Before they could search, Mrs. Claus rounded the hall corner, and Teeny Tiny Elf materialized, instantly sharing with her, "Parv's on it. He said to tell you he completely understands."

Noticing the time travelers had returned, she responded, "Would you go back and let Brennan, Cade, Eanna, Tech Elf, Shorty, and Sarah know Santa's group is back? Ask them to come here so that we can find out together what the group learned."

He glanced at them. "Hi, everybody! I'll be right back!"

"How is Anax?" Santa asked, concerned.

"He's improving. Your assessment of a concussion seems to be accurate," she reported. Turning to her daughter, she continued, "I discovered more about their situation. Not only are they barely surviving on microscopic creatures in the water, but they have placed their children in suspended animation, hoping to find enough food to save them."

"Oh!" Eliza shrieked. "That is awful!"

"Many are not making it. The two who died recently prompted them to seek us out." She halted, her eyes tearing up. "Anax has a child in suspended animation."

"He does?! He also has one that is not," Eliza blurted.

Mrs. Claus nodded. "He relayed how much his little one loves you."

Eliza swiveled to Lugh. "That must be how they kept you guys the days after you disappeared and before Sarah and I were captured."

"No wonder we were hungry!" Lugh exclaimed.

As those from the dome transported in, Mrs. Claus offered, "I'll make us a bite to eat while we share what we have learned the past hours."

"More of your food!" Eanna cried. "Yum!"

"I'll help you, Mother," Eliza offered.

Picking up on Teeny Tiny Elf's message, Santa wondered, "What is Parv doing?"

"I'm having him mix more substance into the water, experimenting to alleviate their hunger," Mrs. Claus replied. "I thought Anax and Doolin could try various concoctions while we work on how to remove the layer."

Santa gave her a big hug followed by a loving kiss. "Thank you, Dear. I have a feeling the Growing Grounds' staff is about to expand their sharing to an interplanetary level."

"Tell us what you found," she encouraged.

As Santa settled into his chair, Mrs. Claus and Eliza turned to meal preparations. When he finished relating the visit to Fitzsimmons and his wife and the group's observations of the planet, he asked, "Did I miss anything?"

The other five shook their heads.

Navva was eager to review what they had discovered from the energy. "Merlin and I had a fascinating discussion with the two clumps of energy, right, Merlin?"

Before Merlin could comment, Navva continued, "One was from plants, and the other was from animals."

"The animals were dependent upon those plants for survival. When the plants died, the animals followed," Merlin recapped.

"That's why they clumped together. The energy from both felt comfortable with each other," Navva added.

"Our two groups were very similar," Lugh expounded. "They also had had an interdependent relationship during their lives on the planet."

"That's what we found, too," Eliza chimed in. "They were shocked to understand how the layering had continued to its present situation."

"Our two groups were willing to move on. How about yours Lugh, Doolin, Navva, and Merlin?" Santa wondered.

The four all nodded and murmured assent.

Santa turned his attention to Tech Elf, Shorty, Sarah, Cade, Brennan, and Eanna, "How are you progressing on the structure?"

"The water babies collected all the parts," Cade reported.

"We've laid it all out in the correct order," Eanna acknowledged.

Santa detected a problem. "What's wrong?"

"Tech Elf had mentioned the material being different," Brennan replied. "He's right. We don't know how to make the pieces adhere to each other."

Lugh smiled at his good friend. "Whenever I encounter that situation, Santa always solves it for me."

Santa smiled back. "Let's look at it after we eat."

Remembering the apparatus construction, Eliza

volunteered, "I'm coming along to learn what Dad does. I never know when I might need it."

Glancing at Eliza, Tech Elf concurred, "Good idea!" He paused. "Sarah, Shorty, and I discovered unknown technology in the AIs and the instrument panels. Despite that, we feel quite confident they are in working order, right?"

Eliza did us a big favor encasing each in an energy exchanger, Sarah noted. *Water would not have been good for them.*

"She's right," Shorty agreed.

Merlin returned to the tough question. "How do we dissipate the layer of energy?"

Santa bounced the question back to Merlin. "What do you recommend?"

"I'm concerned about releasing the energy too fast and creating a tighter backup. We seem to have identified three areas where we could begin untangling the layer. How do we restrain the energy behind from moving too quickly and causing a worse mess?" Merlin queried.

As Santa heard his own worry voiced, he had an epiphany. "Angels!" Without explaining further, he called Joy. "Joy, would you join us, please?

She quickly appeared. Noticing Lugh and Doolin, she was about to comment when Santa offered, "I will give you the entire story which explains Lugh and Doolin."

He did. When he finished, Eliza jumped in. "The water babies on the planet shared with me that they have not seen their angel for a long time. Are you aware of an angel missing a planet?"

Joy sighed. "Sadly, more than one."

"We were discussing how to eliminate the layer by creating openings through which the clogged energy can escape into the ether. Today we visited the planet and went back in time to watch it progress to it current condition. We located three of the initial blockage points and spoke with the energy in them. It was willing to move. We need to have a smooth exit to avoid choking those points. Would angels help us?" Santa asked.

"We would be glad to do that," Joy responded. "We have found the same situation elsewhere and not figured out how to release the energy."

Reading her dad's mind, Eliza was having difficulty containing her excitement. He had a brilliant plan! Forcing herself to focus, she zipped her lips.

"My thought is to position one of us who made contact with the three energy points today at each of those points on the exterior of the layer. Since we are familiar to the energy, it will more readily communicate with us. Another wizard will be at the point on the inside. Doolin, you will stay away. This may be too difficult for you to handle. Mrs. Claus will take your place, okay?"

At Doolin's nod, Santa continued, "Two angels assisting us on the inside and two on the outside of each opening would help to maintain an even flow of the energies' exit. Would twelve angels join us?"

"I'm certain of that," Joy agreed. "The first after me to volunteer will be the one missing contact with her water babies."

A huge humming announced the sylphs. "We'll help, too," the leader stated.

"I was planning on you," Santa returned. "We need as many of you as possible positioned on the exterior of each exit to help the energy into the ether."

Merlin had been absorbing Santa's idea. "How do we get a wizard positioned on the interior of the three points?"

Santa turned to his daughter. He knew she had been restraining herself. "Eliza?"

He was aware that she had already zoomed ahead of his explanation to contemplate that challenge. "I don't think at this point in time we can enter through those three locations from the outside. They are too blocked. If we return to the planet via the structure, I'm hoping the energy inside will separate enough to make a path for us. I had several interactions with those who were trapped inside and think they will help."

Merlin smiled broadly. "We will rely on your charm to make it happen."

Navva seemed annoyed. "Do you want me on the inside with you?"

Eliza detected his feeling and was perplexed. Where did that come from? Instead of answering directly, she deferred to her dad. "I think so, right, Dad?"

Santa discerned a bit of jealousy emanating from Navva. What was that? Was he jealous of Merlin? Out loud, he replied, "Certainly. Merlin would rather not squeeze through trapped energy, right?"

"I appreciate the easy route."

"You, Lugh, and I will be on the exterior of the layer," Santa explained. "Mrs. Claus, Eliza, and Navva will handle the inside." He turned to the sylphs. "Can you squeeze through the energy into the planet side of the layer?"

"How many of us?"

"Three would be enough," Santa returned. "If one of you could get through at each point, those individuals could lead Mrs. Claus, Eliza, Navva, and the angels on the inside to the locations."

They huddled together for a bit, discussing Santa's suggestion. Finally, the lead sylph gave an uncertain answer. "That energy is tight. We'll do our best, but we cannot guarantee that we can penetrate it."

"Even if only one could break through, that individual could possibly lead each of us to one of the points," Eliza offered.

"How does the one, or more, let us know it or they are inside?" Navva questioned.

Eliza looked at him, thinking. "We know that we cannot transport or send telepathy through the energy layer. I was able to communicate telepathically with the eyes located outside the dome but inside the layer, and the Nona residents use telepathy inside all the time. Once the sylphs are inside, I think they could reach us telepathically."

"Okay, let's assume the sylphs can get in and you can communicate with them," Merlin recapped. "How do we know when the structure and, therefore, you have arrived at the planet? When do we start this process? Until we clear the layer, we cannot reach those of you inside."

I'll go back to the planet in the structure with Mrs. Claus, Eliza, and Navva, Sarah replied. *Tech Elf, Shorty, and I will rig up a way through the AIs or the instrument panels for us to alert you when we are there.*

Merlin looked at Tech Elf. "Will you be able to reply? How do we synchronize our efforts?"

"We will set up a reply mode," Tech Elf assured him.

Santa directed a question to Doolin. "Does the dome have an exit to outside?"

Doolin shook his head. "When we conceived of the dome, we did not want to go outside. We wanted protection from the outside and everyone there."

Eliza was stunned. "You mean the only exit is through the water?"

"Yes."

Recovering, Eliza looked at her mother and Navva. "The water isn't deep and doesn't have wave action. Can you both swim in that?"

"I can," Mrs. Claus replied.

"I can, too…I think," Navva agreed, blushing. "Teacher didn't think swimming was important."

"Mother and I will help you," Eliza comforted him. "I met friendly water babies in it who will also help." She paused. "That reminds me, Joy, six of the angels will need to accompany us in the structure. Currently, that is the only way to access the inside for any being, even spiritual ones."

"Oh, that's right! I remember that from Santa's telling what happened. Thanks for mentioning it. I will find out who wants to accompany Santa and who wants to go with us. When are you executing this plan?"

Silence ensued.

Chapter 5

Santa was just about to reply when Anax entered the kitchen. Eliza hastily offered him her seat and moved to another. *How are you feeling?* Santa asked.

Better. He looked at Mrs. Claus. *That last drink was tasty and very satisfying.*

Would you like more? She asked.

Yes, please.

We were just discussing how to dissipate into the ether the layer of energy surrounding your planet, Santa explained.

Anax stared at Eliza. *You are really doing that?*

She nodded. *Yes.*

Santa described their plan to Anax, ending with a question. *Are you up to piloting the structure back home?*

It fell apart.

49

The water babies rescued all the pieces, and we are in the process of assembling it, Santa detailed.

Hope rose in Anax. He might see his family again! Tears flowing out all nine eyes, he answered, *I am.* His gaze shifted to Mrs. Claus. *That drink has given me more strength than I have had in a long time. Thank you.*

I want to know what works for you and your clan. We will have some with us and bring more for everyone as soon as we open up the planet to transport.

Anax was overwhelmed. He had not known this level of attention. Too overcome to respond, he turned his head and noticed Joy. Sliding off the chair and dropping to his knees, he communicated, *An angel! You are an angel!*

I am, Joy replied. *We have come to help you.*

You have come to help us?! Anax repeated, incredulous.

Yes, six of us will help those inside exit smoothly. Once they are outside, six more angels will assist them to move away from the planet into the ether, Joy explained.

Helping Anax get reseated, Santa answered Joy. "We must finalize several critical parts before we proceed. How do we adhere the pieces of the structure together? How do Tech Elf, Sarah, and Shorty rig up a communication system? How fast can the staff at the dome create more of Mrs. Claus's concoction?" He paused. "Contact the angels and let us know when you are ready. We'll give you an update then."

"Talk to you soon," Joy replied. Before disappearing, she enveloped Anax in her loving essence. *I will see you and your clan later.*

Anax's tears flowed out of every eye.

"Let's go to the dome," Santa directed and transported the entire group.

They found the structure's pieces neatly laid out in order down the beach. "Cade, Brennan, Eanna, and Lugh, hold the first pieces together the way they need to connect. Eliza, come with me. We will address how to adhere them. Once we have that, you and I can connect them as the guys hold them up."

"We're headed to my lab to set up a communication system," Tech Elf declared as he and Shorty disappeared along with Sarah.

"Teeny Tiny Elf, come with me to talk to Parv about my concoction," Mrs. Claus instructed.

Doolin and Anax stood to the side, mesmerized. Merlin and Navva stayed beside them.

Santa explained to Eliza what they were about to do. "Similar to the energy exchanger, describe to the energy near the pieces what you want to accomplish. Ask it to attach to where you indicate on the piece. Do the same with the piece to which you want to connect. Then ask the two to bond tightly together. Follow my telepathy as I do two pieces."

First Santa elicited the attention of the energies near two pieces. Then he detailed what he wanted the energies to do. Once the energies agreed, each positioned onto a piece and held fast. Santa moved the two pieces together and used his energy to introduce the two. When they clung together, he backed off and thanked the energies for their help.

"That's similar to how you put the apparatus in place and had it sync with the water's energy!" Eliza exclaimed.

Santa smiled. "Yes. I'm proud that you were able to do that, Daughter, and eager to see your work."

"I wasn't successful on my first attempt," she admitted. "Your voice in my head from training sessions urged me to try again."

"I'm pleased my encouragement stays with you and crosses over into other efforts." Santa turned to the crew. "How is that holding?"

All four pulled on the two pieces. They held tight. "That's good," Lugh announced.

"Okay. Lugh and Eanna, go with Eliza to the end and work toward us. Cade, Brennan, and I will continue to assemble from this end," Santa directed.

Eliza was nervous with her first pieces, which took her three attempts to hold fast. She was thankful for Lugh and Eanna's patience. "Sorry to be so slow," Eliza apologized.

"Your dad wasn't always this fast," Lugh consoled.

She grinned. "Thanks for the reassurance."

After that she picked up speed, and they were close to the halfway mark when they reached Santa's group. "Good work, everyone!" Santa praised. "Now Eliza, Lugh, and Eanna, check what we have done and we will do the same with yours."

I hope ours all hold, Eliza thought, not wanting to embarrass Lugh and Eanna. All the pieces did. So did Santa's.

"Nice work!" Santa concluded. "Having two groups made the job go very fast."

Simultaneously, Mrs. Claus and Teeny Tiny Elf returned and so did Tech Elf, Sarah, and Shorty. "We decided to use technology we already had," Tech Elf related, "instead of attempting to figure out theirs and risk having a new creation not work."

"That's wise," noted Eliza.

We're all set! Sarah finalized

"So is the structure," Santa added. "You can load the instrument panels, your communication system, and the AIs."

"Parv and the staff here are quickly producing more of my concoction. By the time we dissipate the layer into the ether, they'll be ready to transport quite a bit," Mrs. Claus reported.

"We're coming back to let them know when they can do that," Teeny Tiny Elf chirped.

As Merlin and Navva watched the structure being assembled, they had an interesting conversation with Anax and Doolin, learning a great deal about what had happened to the planet and its inhabitants.

Mrs. Claus interrupted their conversation. "We have six ten gallon containers we'd like to take in the structure to help your clan upon our arrival." Looking from Santa to Anax, she continued, "Can the structure handle that weight?"

Santa shifted his gaze to Anax, who nodded. *Spread them throughout so that one part is not bogged down.*

Addressing Cade, Brennan, Eanna, Lugh, Navva, and Merlin, Santa directed, "Let's get the instrument panels in and help Tech Elf and Shorty hook them up. Then load Mrs. Claus's containers, placing them throughout to balance the load." He asked everyone, "Do we want to go now or wait until tomorrow?"

"Since time is of the essence for those on the planet,"

Eliza remarked, "especially the children in suspended animation, let's go now!"

Everyone concurred.

Cade noted, "If you don't mind, we'll wait here and relax on the beach. We'd love to help transport your concoction, Mrs. Claus, as soon as it is possible. We informed our families we'd be home tomorrow. We're not in a rush to get home today."

Eliza's eyes twinkled. "Admit it. You are hoping for two more of Mother's meals, aren't you?"

"That had crossed our minds," Brennan confessed.

"Time on the beach and two more of Mrs. Claus's meals," Eanna noted. "Who would turn that down?"

As the six hauled the instrument panels into the structure, Santa telepathically requested Scott, Violet, and Blogger Elf to join them. Maria tagged along, uninvited. Santa gave them a brief synopsis of the return earlier, what they had done since, and the effort upon which they were about to embark. "In case you are unable to reach us, Violet and Scott, I wanted you to know where we are," Santa concluded. "Blogger, would you please tell the elves that we are gone and what we are doing?"

"I'll be glad to," she answered.

"Tech Elf and Shorty will be monitoring our progress. Check with them if you have any questions," he added.

"Is Navva going with you?" Maria cried, anxious.

Just then Navva exited from the structure. Maria hurried up to him, grabbed him by the arm, and shrieked, "You're not going with them!"

Navva was embarrassed. "Yes, I am, Mother. Please take your hand off my arm."

"No!" She relentlessly carried on. "You do not belong with these wizards. You are not of their caliber. You can't handle what they can. You will die!"

He was flummoxed. Violet and Scott came to his rescue. "Maria," Violet mumbled, "let's go home." Prying Maria's hand off Navva's arm, the three of them disappeared in transport.

Navva looked around at everyone. "I apologize for Mother's outburst. She gets overly concerned about me."

The arrival of twelve angels broke the awkward silence. "You are just in time," Eliza welcomed. "We are almost finished loading the structure."

Their brightness lit up the dome. "We're ready when you are," Joy offered.

Another angel approached Eliza. "I am Evelyn, the angel of the water babies you referenced. Thank you for your concern about them. I am thrilled to see them again. How is Boris?"

"He's fine. When I was knocked unconscious in the water during construction of the apparatus, he saved me. I am eternally grateful to him," Eliza related.

"As are we," Mrs. Claus added.

Tech Elf and Shorty exited the structure. "We have the instrument panels all hooked up and operating smoothly," Tech Elf reported. "The AIs will enter with Anax and Doolin."

"Our communication system appears to be functioning correctly, too," Shorty noted.

"Are Mrs. Claus's concoctions in?" Santa wondered.

As if being called, Parv appeared along with six units. "We took slightly longer to complete these than we anticipated. Sorry for the delay."

"That's okay," Mrs. Claus replied. "You and your team have put these together in record time. Thank you for helping those on Nona."

The six each scooped up a unit and entered the structure. "The units are loaded and spread throughout the structure," Navva announced as they came out.

Anax turned to everyone and projected, *Thank you all for your hard work and kindness to help us. I hope you feel the depth of my gratitude.*

We do, Santa assured him.

Doolin, Anax, and the AIs entered the structure first, followed by Sarah, six angels, Mrs. Claus, and Eliza. Teeny Tiny Elf brought up the rear. Eliza noticed him. "What are you doing here?"

"I'm helping pass out Mrs. Claus's concoction while you guys work on the layer," he stated. "I have an important job."

Eliza chuckled. "Yes, you do. They need it badly."

Pointing behind him toward what Santa and Navva had in their arms, Teeny Tiny Elf expounded, "I need those for my job. Mrs. Claus sent one size glass for the children and one for the adults."

Carrying a table and stool, Santa closely followed Teeny Tiny Elf. Navva was last, his arms filled with a bag of glasses. "Here's what you wanted, Dear," Santa noted. Wrapping his arms around his daughter, he gave her a bear hug and a kiss on the check. Moving next to his wife, Santa hugged Mrs. Claus tightly, ending with a loving kiss. "See you at Nona," he whispered in her ear before pulling away.

As Santa backed out of the structure, Teeny Tiny Elf jumped into Eliza's arms. She turned, waving to Santa, Lugh, and Merlin as the entrance sealed shut. Santa had explained to her how to open it upon their arrival. As he launched the structure into the water, he breathed deeply. He had never watched his wife, daughter, Navva, and Teeny Tiny Elf board a craft together. To calm his nerves, he threw protection around the structure for a safe arrival.

"They'll be fine," one of the angels near him whispered in Santa's ear.

He smiled. "Thank you for your confidence."

Suddenly the air around them hummed with sylphs. They weren't alone. "I see you are accompanied by friends," Merlin noted.

"These are the energy bits which left Santa and Mrs. Claus's family members so that they could return home," the lead sylph explained. "We thought the bits could penetrate the layer and open a spot for us to slip through. They were happy to help."

"Excellent idea!" Santa praised. "The structure just left." Glancing at Tech Elf, Santa added, "Now we wait for notification of their arrival."

Eliza's voice boomed through Tech Elf's speakers. "We're moving smoothly though the water. Sarah thought this would be a good time to test the communication system. Am I coming through, Tech Elf?"

"Loud and clear," he replied.

Santa released a sigh. So far they were safe.

Not being able to see out of the structure, they didn't notice the twelve dragons surrounding it as it moved toward the wormhole entrance. When the structure slipped from the ocean into space, the dragons stopped, projecting safe journey thoughts.

See if you can reach Tech Elf from the wormhole, Sarah encouraged.

Eliza chuckled. Sarah was having fun this trip. "Dad, we are in the wormhole, and the structure is traveling smoothly. Anax says we did a good job on reconstruction. Did you get this?"

Tech Elf almost fell over. They were communicating from a wormhole! He didn't think that was possible! "I did," Santa responded. "Tech Elf is speechless that you can reach us from a wormhole."

"Sarah is delighted," Eliza replied, laughter in her voice.

"The dragons just returned. They accompanied you to the wormhole," Santa added. "They also report the structure is doing well."

"We'll let you know when we arrive," Eliza concluded.

They experienced an uneventful passage through the wormhole. While Anax slid the structure into the dock, Eliza excitedly contacted Santa, "Dad, Merlin, and Lugh, we are here!"

Their reception was garbled, but Tech Elf did detect a message. "I think they've arrived," he announced.

"Tell Eliza we are headed for the outside of the layer," Santa returned.

Tech Elf's reply to Eliza was mostly static, but she assumed he had received her message. "Must be the layer again," she mumbled to Sarah.

When Eliza opened the door, Amir was waiting to greet them. She swung him up and gave him a hug. Passing him to his father, she exclaimed, "We're back with nourishment and help!"

His mother appeared, searching for him. She was astounded to see the structure, her husband, and several others. The angels shocked her. *Angels!* she cried, falling to her knees. *We are saved!*

Her eyes filling with tears, Mrs. Claus helped Anassa stand. *I am Eliza's mother, Mrs. Claus. We have brought nourishment for all of you. Where can we set up six containers so that we can pass it out?*

Anassa was stunned. They had sustenance?! Collecting herself, she pointed, *Along this wall behind me would be good. I will let everyone know.*

She disappeared to alert the others. Navva, Eliza, and Mrs. Claus carried the containers out of the structure and positioned them where Anassa had indicated. With tears of joy flowing down his face, Anax was clutching his child. He was overcome with emotion. For the first time in seemingly forever, his clan would be satiated.

Mrs. Claus positioned Teeny Tiny Elf on a stool next to the small table and unloaded the two sizes of glasses onto the table's top. "I know," he stated before she could repeat her instructions, "Give them one. If they can handle more, give more, but ask first."

She laughed. "That's exactly correct. Thank you."

Glancing down the hall, she noticed the dome. "Is that where you set up the apparatus?" She asked Eliza.

Eliza nodded. "We'll go there as soon as you are ready."

Anassa returned with all the inhabitants behind her. Doolin had gone to bring the leprechauns out, too. Everyone cautiously lined up and, when each one reached Teeny Tiny Elf, accepted the glass that he offered. As they imbibed the liquid, they were pleasantly surprised and returned for more.

Feeling comfortable that Teeny Tiny Elf was handling the process smoothly, Mrs. Claus tucked one arm in Eliza's and one in Navva's. "Let's go!"

Chapter 6

Entering the dome, she halted in amazement. "They tried to copy ours, like you said. I see what you mean about needing more work, though."

The six angels were already in the dome, hovering above the water and communicating with the water babies. Spying Eliza, the water babies all slid onto the shore. "Thank you for bringing our angel! We are thrilled to see her!"

"You are welcome!" Eliza gushed. "We need your help getting out of the dome and onto the shore outside. Can you do that?"

"Sure!" They twittered. "Do the angels want to go, too?"

"Yes." Eliza hesitated. "Wait, though. I want to talk to the eyes outside." Approaching the dome wall, Eliza spoke to the eyes which she knew were there but she couldn't see in the daylight. *We have returned to release you. Three of us and six angels are diving through the water to the shore outside to be with you. We want to make our way up to the atmospheric layer blocking your exit. We have a group already positioned on the outside of the layer, working on creating openings at three locations so that you may leave. Once we get outside the dome, would you help each of us reach one of those openings? We want to make your leaving smooth by managing a continuous stream of spiritual energy through them, avoiding clogs and backups.*

Let a few of us discuss this.

Eliza turned to find her mother and Navva beside her. "We can't see them during the daylight hours, but at night the atmosphere outside is filled with the eyes of the trapped spirits. I came here to describe to them that we need their help to reach the layer. They are discussing how to do that. Could you tap into their telepathy?"

"We arrived by your side just before you noticed us," Mrs. Claus informed her.

"Maybe we'll pick up their answer," Navva added.

They did. *We have suggestions,* the eyes began. *You will be amazed at how tightly together we are packed out here. We are*

64

sending a ripple of telepathy through our midst in order to open a lane for you. The best we can do is one lane which will allow you to proceed one at a time to the layer. Will that work?

Mrs. Claus and Navva nodded. *We will make it work,* Eliza replied. *Each of us will be accompanied by two angels. While they will take less room than us, please allow for the angels, too. Those on the outside of the layer are attempting to slip three sylphs through openings they have created in the layer. One sylph will be positioned inside at each opening.*

Angels?! Angels have come to help us? We are awed. Thank you. Please thank the angels for us. Their presence has a huge effect. We all love and trust angels. The eyes paused. *What are sylphs? We are not familiar with them.*

Air fairies, Eliza explained. *They are very smart, quite small, and enormously helpful.*

We will send a message to watch for them, the eyes returned. *They are a good idea. Their marking the opening helps us identify where to guide you. We will keep the main lane open, but the side ones will close as you reach your destination in order to accommodate the next group of three heading to the layer.*

Okay. We'll join you outside shortly.

Sarah whispered in Eliza's ear, *I'm staying in the dome. I don't want to mix with their energy. I might get swept into the ether. I'll help Teeny Tiny Elf instead.*

Good idea, Eliza noted.

The three returned to the inside shore. "Mother and Navva, I'll create energy exchangers around each of us and each angel." Looking from those two to the angels, Eliza added, "I think we are wise to retain our energy exchangers when we are outside the dome with the eyes in order to give all of us space and Mother, Navva, and me breath, too. What do you think?"

Everyone concurred.

Eliza covered each of them in energy exchangers. She was about finished when Boris popped his head above the water. "Welcome back, Eliza! May I be of assistance?"

She smiled at Navva. "Would you like Boris's help?"

Navva addressed Boris. "I'm not a great swimmer. Would you help me get to the shore?"

"Glad to do that. Join me, and we'll go."

Navva waded in, quickly reaching Boris, and they disappeared. Mrs. Claus and the angels followed with Eliza bringing up the rear. Water babies surrounded and swam beside them, steering them out of the dome, through the open water, and onto a shore of flat rock. When they arrived, the lead water baby advised, "Be prepared to feel squeezed when you enter this outside atmosphere. Spiritual energy consumes it."

The water baby was right. Navva, the first to exit, was able to breathe thanks to the energy exchanger, but he felt pressure. Mrs. Claus and Eliza had the same experience. Suddenly, the eyes telepathically communicated, *We are creating a lane for you to use. Who is first?*

I'll go first, Mrs. Claus volunteered.

She detected an opening of unencumbered atmosphere through which she slowly began to move. Every so often a jostling occurred, and she was bumped around. Sometimes she was squeezed tightly. *Oh! Ouch! Ummm!* She repeated multiple times.

Mother, Eliza asked, concerned. *Mother, are you alright?*

No response.

After a bit, Eliza's request became more urgent. *Mother! Are you okay?*

Remembering Evanescing, Mrs. Claus projected love, joy, and kindness to the spiritual energy around her. *Help me help you* she cycled over and over in her telepathic message to them.

Eliza received her mother's communication, as did Navva. "She's giving off wise emotions and messages," he stated. "I'm copying her when I go."

"You're right," Eliza agreed, relieved.

Finally, Mrs. Claus reached the layer where a sylph

waited. *This way!* The sylph threw over her shoulder as she flew down the lane. Mrs. Claus found the horizontal lane wider and easier going than the vertical one had been. She didn't realize that the lane was closing behind as she and the two angels approached their destination.

Outside, Santa, Lugh, and Merlin had been diligently picking away at the tightly wound energy. When they arrived, they had gone back in time to double-check the coordinates of the locations. Then each positioned himself beside one and began communicating with the energy in order to unravel it. Several sylphs and bits accompanied each of them. The energy bits proved to be invaluable assistants, opening enough space for a sylph to wiggle through to the inside.

Once the three sylphs were in, the bits continued to assist Santa, Lugh, and Merlin by speaking with the energies in the layer and encouraging the separation of any that were able to move. The sylphs outside then escorted that energy into the ether. By the time Mrs. Claus arrived at her position across from Lugh, he, the bits, and sylphs with him had cleared away enough energy for some spiritual energy from the inside to move out. She and the angels immediately recognized the situation and started cautiously urging the spiritual energy through the opening to the waiting sylphs outside.

The angels' presence helped enormously. They commanded the attention, respect, and compliance of the spiritual energy. Mrs. Claus on the inside and Lugh on the outside noticed the flow of exiting energy moving continuously and smoothly, just as they had hoped.

Following Mrs. Claus's example, Navva progressed with less pressure upward to his location across from Santa. Mrs. Claus and the angels with her already seemed to be making a difference in the tightness of trapped energy inside. Santa and the bits with him had created an even larger opening than Lugh's. Recognizing that, Navva and the two angels with him immediately began stimulating the energy near them to slide outward to the waiting sylphs.

Eliza's vertical assent was the fastest. Arriving across from Merlin, she, Joy, and Evelyn quickly achieved a rapid exit of spiritual energy. The sylphs outside had to step up their pace. Some energy dissipated into the ether without help. Everyone on both sides of the layer felt the joy of the energies' release.

As the openings expanded, the flow of energy grew from a trickling stream to a white water rush. The attention of those on both sides of the layer had the desired effect. None of the energy clogged the openings. All maintained an effortless flow.

Soon Mrs. Claus, Navva, and Eliza could see Lugh, Santa, and Merlin. *It's working!* Eliza exclaimed excitedly. *Wow! This is tremendous!*

Parts of the layer began to disappear, and the planet once again became visible. Everyone was so focused on the dissipation of the energy that time seemed to stop. Later they would comment that the energy release was fast, very fast. The last to leave were the eyes outside the dome with whom Eliza had spoken. Emitting waves of gratitude, they halted beside her. *Thank you. Thank you so much for helping us.*

I can feel your thanks, Eliza responded. *You are very welcome.*

We hope you help those left alive, too.

We already are doing that. Mother developed a concoction which gives them more substance than they have been receiving from the water alone. They are imbibing that right now. Since the planet is now open to transport, we will bring them more. Next we will help those in suspended animation.

That's great! We are excited the structure could be used to bring you here twice.

Eliza didn't reveal that they had had to reconstruct it. *We were grateful for it, too.*

With those exchanges, they disappeared into the ether.

"Let's go down to the planet surface," Santa suggested as they grouped together.

"Follow me," Eliza encouraged. "I have an idea of another entry into the dome."

Not certain of the air's composition, all of them retained their energy exchangers. After they settled onto solid ground, Eliza looked at her dad. "This atmosphere responds to wishes. Would you please envision an appropriate entry here and wish it? I trust you to take the inhabitants as well as us into account in your creation."

"Okay."

Everyone bridled their expressions of joy, waiting to share with each other when they were inside.

"Come with me," Santa directed as he stepped back and to his left several paces. They saw a piece of the dome in front of them replaced by a sliding door. "Stay where you are until I move," he added.

An enclosed entry was erected around the outside of the door and toward their group, stopping right in front of them and ending with a sliding door which immediately opened. Santa swept his arm toward the entry, smiling at Eliza. "As you wish, Daughter."

In awe, they moved slowly through the entry, looking closely at the construction and running their hands across it. Lugh turned to his good friend. "Nice work."

"This feels like the structure," Eliza commented.

Santa nodded. "I used the same material, assuming it would handle this atmosphere well."

As they entered the dome, the energy bits, sylphs, and angels surged in alongside them. Mrs. Claus turned to her husband, "I see you brought the walkway up to the entry. Good thinking, Dear." She finished with a loving kiss and a big hug.

Her action released the floodgate of excitement over what they had accomplished. Eliza grabbed her partner on the outside of the layer, Merlin, and gave him a kiss on the cheek followed by a big hug. Next she kissed and hugged Lugh. Then she swiveled to Navva, wrapping her arms around him in a tight hug, whispering "Good job" in his ear, and ending with a loving kiss. She finished with hugs and kisses with her mother and dad. "Thank you, Mother, for leading the way to the layer. You were an excellent example for Navva and me."

Eliza smiled into Santa's eyes. "I knew you could do it, Dad. As usual, you have verified my complete confidence in you."

"Don't minimize your contribution, Daughter," he replied. "Your thinking through what we had to do and returning with Doolin and Anax expedited this effort."

As Eliza gave him another hug, Santa glanced over her shoulder at Navva who appeared unsettled. What was bothering Navva? Santa wondered.

Oblivious to Navva, Mrs. Claus announced, "Let's see how Teeny Tiny Elf is doing."

She dropped her energy exchanger, as did almost everyone else. Teeny Tiny Elf met her by the shore. "You're back! Are you done?" He looked outside and noticed bright light.

"We are," Mrs. Claus answered. "How are you doing?"

"I'm out!"

"You're out?! Really? I thought we had plenty for today."

He shook his head emphatically. "Nope. I'm out! I need more."

Without saying another word, Mrs. Claus hurried to the hall where Nonas and leprechauns were patiently waiting. She instantly contacted Parv. *We have dispersed the layer blocking entrance to the planet. Do you have six more containers of concoction ready? If so, would you immediately transport them to my location? Cade, Brennan, and Eanna offered to help. They are sitting on the beach.*

Be right there.

She had barely received his reply when he and the crew

appeared beside her, each one of the crew overseeing two containers. Teeny Tiny Elf had resumed his seat next to the table. "Take away the first one and set one in its spot," Mrs. Claus advised Parv. Glancing at the crew, she requested, "Would each of you replace an empty with a full one and take the empties back to the North Pole?"

More? Anassa cried. *You have more for us?*

Yes, Mrs. Claus answered. *We are making more than that, too.* She looked around for Santa, who was nowhere in sight.

Curious to see his daughter's work, Santa had stopped by the apparatus. Still wearing his energy exchanger, he waded into the water, ducked under the apparatus, and thoroughly examined it. When he was peering closely at the deepest part, Boris appeared next to him. "She did a good job," Boris stated. "It has not hesitated or stopped since she started it."

"You must be Boris," Santa noted. "Thank you for your appraisal and thank you for saving her life."

"She impressed me. Despite being kidnapped and brought here without her consent, she discovered the problem and went further than requested, bringing you, your wife, Merlin, and Navva back to help us."

"That's the way she works."

"Yes. You and your wife must be proud of her."

"Very." Santa paused. "She said you expected her."

"I did, and I know her impact will go far beyond the Project Committee work. We are all thankful for her. Please pass that along to Mrs. Claus, too."

Santa smiled. "We are thankful to have her back."

"She has a tough time coming up, but you have an inkling of that, don't you?"

Not immediately replying, Santa stared at Boris. After a bit, Santa asked, "So what I have been noticing has foundation?"

"Deep roots that must be addressed. The problem will not be ignored," Boris warned.

"Santa? Santa? Are you in the water?" Mrs. Claus called.

With a parting glance, Santa ended their conversation and surfaced. "Yes, Dear."

She looked from him to their daughter standing beside her. "Are we doing more today? Parv just transported another six containers of my concoction. Do I tell them we are coming with more tomorrow?"

"We have had a full day," Santa replied. "I think we are wise to go home, have dinner, recap today, and plan tomorrow."

By that time he had dissipated his energy exchanger.

"What about the children in suspended animation?" Eliza asked urgently.

"We'll do that tomorrow," Santa replied. He turned to Merlin. "Would you stay over and return with us tomorrow and however many days we need to help those children?"

Merlin nodded. "I'd be glad to do that."

Looking at Navva, Santa caught him giving Merlin an irritated stare. "I assume you will help, too."

Navva changed to a smile. "Sure."

What is Navva's problem with Merlin? Santa wondered. "Good! Are you ready to go home, Dear?"

"I want to give Parv directions and explain our leaving to Anassa. Give me a couple of minutes." She addressed Joy. "The Nona clan would like to thank you, the sylphs, and the energy bits. Would you gather here so that they can do that?"

"I'll get everyone," Joy responded.

"Would you also accompany us back to the North Pole so that you can participate in our recap of today?" Santa requested.

"We angels would love to do that," she gushed. "I'll check with everyone else."

Joy quickly found the sylphs, energy bits, and angels

scattered around the dome. She returned with all of them about the same time Mrs. Claus came back with the entire clan. With tears flowing out of all nine eyes, Anax initiated waves of gratitude toward each being and energy that had helped. Every individual in the clan joined him. The helpers felt engulfed in a sea of gratefulness and returned the appreciation.

The dome reverberated with pure joy.

The wizards and Lugh projected, *See you tomorrow.* Then all the helpers disappeared.

Everyone arrived in Mrs. Claus's kitchen. Eliza started the conversation. "Thank you, energy bits, for your help. You made a huge difference in opening up the layer."

"Yes, thank you," the sylph leader echoed. "You helped tremendously."

"We have other planets that are missing," Joy volunteered. "If we can find them, would you, energy bits and sylphs, help us open them up, too?"

"You are very welcome," one of the energy bits returned. "We were glad to help and would do so again."

"Do you need us tomorrow?" the sylph leader wondered.

Eliza deferred to Santa. "The leprechauns and wizards can handle those in suspended animation," Santa remarked.

"Then we will see you later," the sylph leader replied, disappearing with the energy bits.

"Thank you, angels," Eliza effused. "Your presence today helped get the attention of the spiritual energy and maintain a steady stream through the exits. We appreciate you very much."

"If you would like Joy and me to join you tomorrow," Evelyn offered, "we would be glad to do that."

Santa thought for a second, his brow furrowing. "Depending upon the state of those in suspended animation, your presence might be helpful. That's a good idea." He looked at the other ten. "If we find we need more, may we contact you?"

"Please do," responded one. "If that's all for now, we are off seeking missing planets."

Chapter 7

As those remaining expressed gratitude, the angels vanished. Lugh had stopped at the South and Indian Ocean Dome to pick up Cade, Brennan, and Eanna. They showed up as the angels left. Sarah had swung by the lab and brought Tech Elf and Shorty. For the benefit of those who had not been at the planet, Eliza recounted unraveling the layer and assisting the spiritual energy into the ether.

When she finished, Santa addressed the entire group. "Tomorrow we start waking up those in suspended animation. In every case, a wizard will start the process. We will begin with those who have been in that state the longest. They are the weakest. Remember they were put that way to save them because a good food source did not exist." He turned to Mrs. Claus. "What is the status of more of your concoction?"

"Everyone at the dome, including lots of elves who do not normally work there, is working to produce as much as possible and still maintain the nutrition level we established. When we transport in the morning, we will bring more for those not in suspended animation as well as plenty for those who are in that state," Mrs. Claus reported.

"If you'd like some help, Shorty and I will each bring one," Tech Elf offered.

"Yeah," Shorty chimed in. "We'd like to see this dome and the apparatus Eliza and the crew erected."

I'll tag along and explain everything to them, if that's okay, Sarah offered.

"I'd like all three of you with us, too," Santa noted. "I have a feeling we may have need of your talents."

"Everyone plan to transport one container," Mrs. Claus clarified.

"You will have that many?" Eliza uttered, shocked.

"Yes," her mother verified.

"What process do you want us to use in reviving the children?" Merlin asked.

"Start by giving a child energy at a level you detect that individual can handle—"

"Dad," Eliza interrupted, "In that state, Lugh, Cade, Eanna, Brennan, and I floated with no support. I suspect we will find the children doing the same. We fell to the floor when we were released. For the children's sake, we may want to materialize a cushion of some sort on which to place them."

He smiled lovingly at his daughter. "Good point. Thank you, Eliza. Start by materializing a cushion for the child. As you give the child energy, gently lower the individual to settle on the softness. Continue to project small amounts of energy. Don't give too much. Instill the energy slowly. Watch closely and adjust as needed. Remember, these are children. Begin with a very small amount. You will be performing a touchy procedure, especially with those who have been in suspended animation the longest. Work on one at a time. When the child comes out of suspended animation, offer Mrs. Claus's concoction. Each of us will have either Lugh, Cade, Brennan, Eanna, or Teeny Tiny Elf helping. Once you feel the child is awake and stable, have the one helping you handle the child, and you move on to the next one," Santa instructed.

"Joy and Evelyn," Santa singled out. "Would you keep an eye on the wizards? If you notice one of us having difficulty waking up a child, would you help? You had an extremely fortuitous presence today in sustaining a steady exit at the layer. Likewise, you may be instrumental in reviving these children calmly."

They both glowed brightly in agreement.

"Lugh, Cade, Brennan, Eanna, and Teeny Tiny Elf, one of you will help each wizard. As I just mentioned, once the child is awake and stable, you will encourage the individual to imbibe Mrs. Claus's concoction at the appropriate rate. Teeny Tiny Elf, after we have dinner, would you please instruct the other four on that rate?"

"Will do, Santa!"

Santa smiled. "Thank you." He looked at those five. "When you feel comfortable the child is absorbing the sustenance at a suitable rate, have a Nona or leprechaun who is available to help assume that function and you follow the wizard to the next child."

All five nodded understanding.

"Any questions?" Santa concluded.

"What happens to the children once they are stabilized? Will the Nona move them somewhere else? The Nona and the leprechauns helping must need to follow the wizard, too. Who handles the child when they do that?" Navva wondered.

"Good question, Navva," Merlin praised.

"Yes, good question," Santa repeated. Glancing at Tech Elf, he asked, "Can you program Cookie Robot to carry or lead, depending upon the individual's condition, a child to another location? Could you do the same with the AIs that ran the structure?"

Tech Elf quickly assessed the process. "We need five to match the five wizards and their five assistants Teeny Tiny Elf, Lugh, Cade, Brennan, and Eanna." He looked at Shorty. "I think we can, right?"

Shorty nodded. "We can reprogram Cookie tonight and the two AIs once we arrive tomorrow."

"You and I can be the fourth and fifth," Tech Elf noted.

"Don't feel rushed," Santa inserted. "Reviving the children may be a slow process."

His words proved prophetic.

None of the group from the North Pole had asked how many children were in suspended animation. When the door to the area holding the children was opened, the wizards, leprechauns, elves, and even Shorty were stunned. The area seemed endless. All they could see everywhere were floating little Nonas and leprechauns.

"Oh, my goodness," Mrs. Claus cried softly.

Santa turned to Anax. *How many?*

Anax sadly returned, *About three hundred.*

Eliza gasped. She and the rest of the helpers felt the enormity of the situation and the severity of the risk to the clan's survival. Anax and the leprechauns were literally on the brink of extinction.

Santa continued his exchange with Anax. *Which have been here the longest?*

Anax led them to the furthest part of the room. *We started here to leave plenty of room for additions. We never imagined we would fill it.*

Is that why your younger child is not here? You don't have room? Eliza wondered.

Yes. He stopped by one of the furthest children. This is our older child. He looked at Santa. *Would you do your best with him? He is extremely weak.*

Without replying, Santa materialized a cushion on the floor. Sliding his arms underneath the child, Santa tenderly sent the child tiny waves of energy. Anax positioned himself on his child's other side. As the floating function dissipated, Santa gently lowered the child onto the softness and knelt down beside him.

Everyone else was mesmerized watching Santa perform an example of the awakening process. The wizards were keenly noting Santa's steps. After what seemed an eternity, the child opened one eye, seeing Santa and noticing Joy hovering over his shoulder. When the child turned to see his father, his eye brightened. Anax lovingly stroked his son's face, projecting love and reassuring him that Santa was a helper.

Inspired, Mrs. Claus requested of Anassa, *Would you be certain a parent is helping us with his or her child? Similar to the angel, the parent's presence will calm the child.*

Tears spilling down her face, Anassa replied, *I will. Thank you for helping our son first.* She left to inform all the parents.

Santa continued to instill energy into the child. When the child opened all nine eyes at once, Santa attempted to give him a bit of the concoction. He refused to imbibe it. Extending the glass to Anax, Santa urged, *You offer it to him. He trusts you.*

Accepting the glass from Santa, Anax absorbed some concoction so that the child could see his father doing so. That made the difference. The child tried some, too.

They all held their breath, hoping the child handled the concoction well. Santa waited quite a while, and the child seemed fine so Santa moved on to the next child. The other wizards along with their helpers each sought out their first ones.

Santa had just slipped his hands underneath the next child when Anax urgently summoned Santa back. *My boy is not responding! Help!*

Immediately returning, Santa knelt down beside Anax's child. He did not react. Santa gently picked up the boy's limp body, drew him close, and cradled him like a baby, all the while trickling sparkles of energy into his body. Santa was oblivious as to how long he remained in that position. His goal was to save the child.

Everyone else returned to watch. They wanted to learn from Santa what to do.

They did not know if the child would survive.

When the child twitched and then opened one eye slightly, Santa smiled into the boy's eye. *How do you feel?* Santa projected.

I *was so weak... Have you been helping me feel stronger?*

I have. Do you feel stronger?

Yes. What did I take? It was good.

Something we made specially to help you and your family.

Thank you. The child closed his eye. When he reopened it, he asked, *How are the other children?*

We are working on waking them up. You were the first one.

I was first? He paused. *Thank you for doing that for me and my family.*

You are welcome, Santa responded. *If you feel strong enough,*

I'll leave you with your dad and tend to another child.

The boy opened three eyes and turned to his dad. *Hi, Dad! I thought I remembered seeing you before.* He glanced back at Santa. *I think I am strong enough now. If I'm not, Dad will let you know, right, Dad?*

With tears running down his face, Anax accepted his son from Santa. *Hold him for a while,* Santa advised. *His energy will be stabilized by your calm reassurance.*

Standing, Santa turned to Merlin, Mrs. Claus, Eliza, and Navva. "What you just witnessed may be typical. Be prepared to give each child energy in tiny bits, keep an eye on the children you have awakened, and return promptly if necessary. During the gap between their waking up and the absorption of the concoction into their systems, they may relapse, which will require your attention. The children who have been here the longest will be the trickiest to revive. As you just saw, they are very weak."

"What were the sparkles?" Eliza wondered.

"Droplets of energy that upon entering his body became readily absorbable fluid," Santa answered. He described how to produce them. "Any questions?" He finished.

"Why do that?" Navva queried.

"Beings in his condition may be too weak to take in

pure energy, even in tiny bits. Receiving the energy as fluid might be more acceptable to his body right now," Santa explained.

Feeling they had a complete understanding of what they were facing, the wizards and their helpers each selected a child to awaken. They encountered the same situation as Santa, which made their progress very slow the first day. Each wizard revived three children, except Santa who brought back four. By the end of the day, the wizards were exhausted and low on energy. They enjoyed Mrs. Claus's dinner and with little discussion went into Dreamland.

Lugh, Cade, Brennan, and Eanna wanted to continue to help until all the children were awakened. Before dinner, each contacted their families and informed them of the delay. Their family members expressed shock at the situation and applauded them for helping.

The next two days continued similar to the first. Every child was touch and go. Many had to be attended at least twice, sometimes three times. After three days of intense effort, each wizard had brought back nine children. The wizards were not bothered by the slow pace. They were thrilled that in every instance they had successfully revived the child.

On the fourth day Santa asked the other ten angels to return. As the wizards' rate of revival picked up, the angels' presence proved invaluable. They and the parents made a significant difference in calming, stabilizing, and strengthening the children. The fourth, fifth, and sixth days each wizard revived six children per day.

Whether the later children's condition was less fragile or the wizards had become more proficient, the wizards stepped up the pace to eleven per day on days seven, eight, and nine when they finished. Thankfully, the first six days had given the AIs a great deal of practice. They applied all they had learned during the last three days, steadily carrying the children to a comfortable place to rest and be given attention.

A couple times Navva expressed frustration at his feelings of incompetence while awakening children. In his view, all the other wizards were much better and faster at revival than him. He seemed inferior alongside Merlin, Santa, and Mrs. Claus. Although not true, he was particularly concerned how inadequate he appeared to Eliza. He wanted to measure up to her, her parents, and Merlin's level. Over and over in his mind, he heard his mother screaming, "You are not their caliber!"

Despite that, Navva kept up, successfully awakening as

many children as everyone else. With each one, he found enormous satisfaction and realized he loved children. He started thinking about having his own. Before that he had not entertained the idea.

When Navva finished awakening the last child on the ninth day, everyone else cheered. They were on a high at being able to revive all the children. As the AIs carried the child out, the room filled with Nonas and leprechauns. Once they were all inside, Anax expressed, *We are overcome with gratitude at your efforts to revive our children and keep them alive. Thank you very much.*

Their waves of thankfulness enveloped the helpers, adding to the helpers' joy.

We are overjoyed that all of them survived. Santa returned. *With several, particularly at the start, we were not certain of a positive outcome, but time after time our teams pulled the children through. I join you in applauding the helpers.* While he made the last statement, Santa turned, faced all the helpers, and clapped heartily.

Stepping next to Santa, Mrs. Claus added, *Thank you. We all appreciate your gratitude. We will be back with more of my concoction tomorrow. Right now I am taking these helpers home and making them a celebration dinner.* Tucking her left arm around Santa, she raised her hand to wave to the clan but dropped it and pressured Santa with her other hand to delay transporting.

Eliza had skirted around the crowd and was leaving the room. Mrs. Claus couldn't see Amir leading her daughter. While everyone was focused on the exchange of thanks, he had tugged on Eliza's pant leg. She had smiled brightly at him. *Hi!*

Come with me. I want you to see something.

Grabbing her hand, he led her out of the room and down the hall toward the dome. As they neared, she could hear quite a commotion. She'd not heard some of the sounds before, but they included splashing. Rounding the corner into the dome, she immediately viewed the source of the noise. Hundreds of Nona and leprechaun children were having fun splashing in the water. They were getting themselves and each other wet, emitting what for them was laughter.

Amir pulled her to the shore where she had introduced him to the water. He knelt down, filled his hand with water, and tossed it in Eliza's face. She laughed heartily, stooped down, and returned the action to him. By the time Santa, Mrs. Claus, Navva, Merlin, Teeny Tiny Elf, and the crew arrived, Eliza's shirt was soaked. She had plunked down on the beach and was tossing water at every child she could reach.

Teeny Tiny Elf squeezed past everyone and joined the fun. Hopping to Eliza's left, he showed the children new techniques to splash the water on others including some he had learned from fairies.

Delighting in the happiness of the children, Santa didn't notice Amir's older brother, the first child Santa had revived, sneak up on Santa and pour water all over his shoes. Chuckling, Santa scooped the child up and waded into the water, giving him a full water dousing. As the child surfaced, he threw water in Santa's face. Both laughed heartily.

Soon the water babies showed up, sliding onto the beach into the middle of the fun. They put on a special show for the children after which the kids resumed their splashing. Navva, Merlin, and the crew followed Eliza's example. Before the helpers left, every one, even Santa and Mrs. Claus, was soaked.

The interaction on the beach between the kids, their helpers, and the water babies turned into a big celebration of reviving the children. As they gathered for transport, Amir stretched his arms for Eliza to pick him up. *Will you come back to visit me?*

Her eyes welling up with tears, Eliza smiled. *I will be here a lot.* Finishing with a kiss on his cheek and a big hug, she set him down, waving as she disappeared in her dad's transport.

When they arrived in Mrs. Claus's kitchen, she immediately looked at Eliza and Navva. "Would you two help me, please?"

"Glad to," Navva replied before Eliza could say a word.

She smiled at him. "What would you like us to do?"

Following Mrs. Claus's assignments, the three had dinner prepared in record time. After the first taste, Cade released a sigh of contentment. "A huge bonus the past ten days has been your meals, Mrs. Claus. Thank you. If you don't mind, I'm staying for breakfast."

Mrs. Claus chuckled. "Thank you, Cade. You are welcome at breakfast tomorrow."

Lugh glanced at the rest of the crew. "I think we are all staying."

"Count me in," Merlin contributed. "I'll use my sleeping arrangement one more night for a Mrs. Claus breakfast. How long are you planning to feed the clan?"

"As long as necessary," she replied. "We have set up a program to keep my concoction flowing to them. With the children revived, we have increased the amount. Tomorrow morning I am meeting with the heads of the domes to discuss how to proceed. We want to gradually increase the amount of plant food in their diets. We are also planning to revise the interior of the dome by including more plants and places for the children to play." She glanced at Santa. "When we run out of space, Santa will construct another dome with the crew's help, right, Dear?"

Santa looked at Eliza. "We may have an easy time since I just have to wish it."

"Let's have Eliza insert the apparatus," Lugh offered.

"Great idea!" Santa responded. "She did an excellent job installing the one in the current dome."

Eliza blushed. "Since you hadn't said anything after checking it out, I assumed I made mistakes that you wanted me to correct but hadn't had time to explain."

Santa wrapped his arm around his daughter, who was sitting next to him. "You're right; I have been busy. I scrutinized it closely. You did a beautiful job, especially considering you received my instructions second-hand."

She kissed him on the cheek. "Thanks, Dad. Your approval means a great deal to me."

"How far are you on the leprechaun book?" Lugh wondered.

"We kept all the appointments you and Rosy had scheduled," Eliza returned, "and I had been keeping up with writing it. I would like to insert recent events. Do you have more you want to include?"

Lugh thought a moment. "No," he responded slowly. "I think Rosy and I had covered the aspects I wanted. I asked because I wondered when to hold the meeting about the manuscript."

"Does three weeks work?" Eliza offered. "I have a few clients who need my attention, and I want to review and finish the book."

"Three weeks it is!" Lugh echoed enthusiastically.

Eliza turned to her mother. "Yes, Dear," Mrs. Claus volunteered, knowing Eliza's request. "Teeny Tiny Elf and I will bring lunch. Let me know the exact date."

Remembering an addition to the book, Eliza swung back to Lugh. "As I was writing, I had a question of you. I want to talk about that when we get home."

He glanced at Santa. "I hope it doesn't involve your dad."

She looked at her dad and smiled.

Chapter 8

Their plans for the next day were about to change. Everyone had just settled down for the night when Mrs. Claus and Eliza received an urgent telepathic message from Fiona. *Meet me at Eliza's house immediately. Leave Santa at home. Transport separately from each of your rooms. Do not let anyone except Santa know you left.*

Curious, both followed Fiona's instructions. Mrs. Claus related the exact message to Santa. Giving him a loving kiss, she smiled. "I'll be back shortly, Dear."

His brow furrowed. "What is urgent this time of the night?"

"I'll let you know when I return."

They arrived simultaneously in Eliza's lighted kitchen. Fiona was anxiously waiting. Behind her they noticed tuxedos in varying sizes neatly spread all over the living room. She blurted out the question consuming her. "Are you finished reviving the children on Nona?"

"Yes, we brought the last one out of suspended animation today," Mrs. Claus replied.

"Are they all okay?"

Both Mrs. Claus and Eliza nodded. "We are thrilled that all of them made it," Eliza shared. "They treated us to a splashing party in the water before we left."

Fiona's shoulders noticeably dropped. "What a relief! I am very glad to hear they are all okay. If they weren't, I was ready to call off tomorrow's event."

"What event?" Eliza wondered.

Fiona breathed deeply. "You remember what I said about moving in with Lugh when he returned?"

"We do," Mrs. Claus responded. "Have you?"

"Well, yes," Fiona confessed, "but that's not why I summoned you here at this hour. I have planned a hand-fasting for Lugh and me. I calculated when you might be finished reviving the children and selected tomorrow. I have secretly planned the occasion, set it up with the help of your neighbors, Eliza, and invited guests. Your attention to the children took longer than I had anticipated. I was very nervous that I had chosen the wrong date."

Mrs. Claus wrapped her arms around Fiona. "Oh, Fiona! I am so excited for you and Lugh!"

Eliza echoed her mother's expression of joy. As soon as Mrs. Claus pulled away, Eliza hugged Fiona tightly. "Welcome, neighbor! I am thrilled for you both and delighted to have you living close by!"

"Thank you for your excitement and support," Fiona sighed. "As I mentioned when you interviewed me, Eliza, I was determined not to leave Lugh alone anymore. I didn't want just to move in. I wanted to make our arrangement official with a hand-fast—"

Ever the inquisitive mind, Eliza interrupted, "Is that what leprechauns call marriage?"

Fiona nodded. "Yes. I intended to surprise Lugh by having it all set. I did not intend to make it this much of a surprise, but I didn't want to interrupt your work on the children. I apologize for rousting you out of Dreamland. I couldn't come up with a better way to handle what we are about to discuss."

"Neither one of us was in Dreamland, yet, were we, Eliza?" Mrs. Claus assured Fiona. "What can we do to help?"

Addressing Eliza, Fiona answered, "Would you have Lugh transport home with you?" Stepping over to the nearest tuxedo, she continued, "Explain to him what is about to happen and have him put this on?"

Remembering the guys taking a dip in the water at Nona, Eliza smiled mischievously. "I'll be happy to do that. Where do you want me to bring him?"

"I have chosen the Little Tree for our hand-fasting."

Tears welled up in Eliza's eyes. "Oh, that is an excellent choice. The Little Tree will be thrilled!" She paused. "Wait…teach me about a leprechaun marriage. You hold the ceremony in front of a tree?"

"Or a favored shrub. Generally a hawthorn or rowan is selected. The little tree has such significance to Lugh, you, and your family that I felt it was the best choice."

Eliza could not resist giving Fiona another hug. "Thank you. I am overwhelmed with your consideration."

"Yes, thank you," Mrs. Claus repeated.

"You are welcome. I'm glad you approve." Sighing again, Fiona gestured to the other tuxedoes. "I have one for Santa, Teeny Tiny Elf, Merlin, Navva, Cade, Brennan, and Eanna. Would you take them home with you and have the guys put them on before they arrive?"

"Merlin?" Eliza exclaimed. "How did you get his measurements?"

Fiona grinned. "I'm not telling."

"Any suggestions on how we keep the guys from leaving without tipping our hand to Lugh?" Mrs. Claus asked.

"Have Santa handle that," Fiona suggested. "He'll come up with an idea." She paused. "Would you also ask Santa to tie the ribbon around our hands? I would be honored to have him perform that role."

"I'm sure **he** will be honored," Mrs. Claus repeated.

"I have so many questions," Eliza remarked, "but I am not bothering you now. I'll get them answered attending the ceremony, I'm sure."

"Can we help you with anything else?" Mrs. Claus offered.

"Your assistance with what we have discussed is a big weight off my shoulders," Fiona revealed. "I have been tortured as to how to reach you, if this will work for you, and what to do as a back-up plan."

"Since Dad, Navva, and Merlin's tuxedoes are a similar size, you take those, Mother," Eliza directed. "I'll take Cade, Brennan, Eanna, and Teeny Tiny Elf's." She had an inspiration. "I can tell Lugh I have an early appointment tomorrow and ask him to transport home with me and the dogs. Once I get him out of the North Pole, you and Dad can tell Navva, Merlin, Teeny Tiny Elf, and the guys. They can change in my bedroom. I'll leave their tuxedoes on my rolling rack."

"Why will Lugh feel he has to go with you?" Fiona questioned.

Eliza's eyes twinkled. "Your guy will usually come with me when I ask."

Fiona smiled back. "I'll remember to enlist your assistance if he resists doing what I request."

Mrs. Claus chuckled. "Poor Lugh. His life is about to change."

All three laughed merrily.

Giving Fiona another hug and a kiss on the cheek, Eliza and Mrs. Claus picked up the tuxedoes they were taking and transported back to the North Pole. "I'll turn off the lights and close up," Fiona stated as they left.

Consumed with curiosity, Santa was waiting for Mrs. Claus. When she appeared holding three tuxedoes, his interest rose to a new height. "What?"

"Fiona has planned her and Lugh's hand-fasting for tomorrow." With that opening statement, she shared the entire visit with her husband. By the time she finished, Santa was chuckling.

"I applaud Fiona's initiative. You're right, Dear. I am honored to tie the ribbon for them. She and Lugh are a good fit. What a celebration!"

As soon as they sat down for breakfast, Eliza mentioned to Lugh, "Checking my calendar last night, I realized I have an appointment scheduled for 8. Would you accompany me home and help me get the dogs settled before I leave?"

He smiled. "Sure. I'd like to see Fiona right away. Going home with you at that time will get me to her place before she starts work."

Eliza, Mrs. Claus, and Santa exercised every bit of constraint they could muster not to laugh or even smile. Unwittingly, Cade fit into the plan. "Merlin, Brennan, and Eanna, let's not rush. I want a leisurely intake of Mrs. Claus's wonderful meal. I know I won't have another for a while."

"Sounds good to me," Merlin concurred.

"Me, too," Brennan and Eanna agreed.

Santa smirked at Eliza. *Thanks for your assist, Daughter. You're welcome, Dad. Anytime.*

Eliza transported them into the back hall at her house. Lugh immediately opened the back door and let Dusty and Chance into the yard. "Sounds like quite a bit of activity out there for an early morning," Lugh noted.

Closing the door, he turned and was engulfed in Eliza's hug. "I am overjoyed for you," she whispered into his ear.

"What–"

Keeping her arms around him and pulling back enough to speak with him face to face, she explained, "Just after we retired into our rooms last night, Mother and I had an urgent message from Fiona to meet her here."

Lugh was shocked. "Why? Is she alright? Is she upset with me?"

He had not seen Eliza smile so broadly. "She has planned and set up your hand-fasting for today beside the Little Tree."

Chance and Dusty began barking at the commotion they heard outside. Stepping around Lugh, Eliza opened the door and called, "Barney, would you please help?"

He materialized in front of her. "I'm on it!" he cried as he ran to play with the dogs.

Swiveling back to Lugh who was stunned speechless, Eliza grabbed his hand and headed for the living room. She stopped in front of the tuxedo. "Fiona made this for you."

Lugh reached out, gently running his hand down the fabric. "This feels like what she would select." He paused, choked up. "Is that what the commotion outside is about?"

"I suspect the dogs are reacting to the guests arriving," Eliza noted.

"I am overcome…"

"When I related my interview of Fiona to you, I left out that she had decided to move in as soon as you returned in order to keep a closer eye on you. Last night she shared that she wanted to make your union official." Eliza halted. "I hope I am communicating my excitement for the two of you, my awe that you have her in your life, and my thrill that she will now be my neighbor."

"Thank you," Lugh returned, giving her a big hug. Teary-eyed, he pulled back. "I suppose I better put this on."

"Do you mind using the bathroom?" Eliza asked. "I'd like to use the bedroom to change into a dress."

Also remembering the incident on Nona, Lugh smiled. "Sure."

"Wait for me in the sunroom. I'll get the dogs in. I don't want them to brush against that gorgeous fabric."

Once Eliza was dressed, she let the dogs in the back door, thanked Barney for his help, and ushered the dogs into the spare bedroom where they wouldn't hear the outside event. "See you later, guys," she bid, closing the door.

Joining Lugh in the sunroom, Eliza escorted him to the Little Tree where Santa was waiting, a broad smile on his face. Eliza stepped into the crowd to stand between her mother and Navva.

Suddenly, the crowd quieted and parted. Wearing a breath-taking dress sparkling with tiny prisms, Fiona strolled down the opening toward Lugh. She had a rose affixed to each of her wrists. When she reached Lugh, she pulled the rose off her right hand and secured it onto his right hand. "I love you, Lugh," she murmured.

"I love you, too, Fiona," he returned, extending his left arm beside her right one toward Santa.

Santa entwined the ribbon around Fiona and Lugh's arms, comfortably binding them together. As he finished, he gently placed his hands over their linked ones. In a booming voice, he expressed, "Hand-fasting Fiona and Lugh is a great pleasure and honor for me. They are tremendous individuals who love each other and belong together. Today we celebrate their union!"

Awkwardly turning as one, Fiona and Lugh managed to face their guests. Amid the crowd's wild cheers, they returned down the opening Fiona had created and established a reception line. All nine bankers were the first to congratulate them. "You all came!" Lugh exclaimed.

The lead one smiled. "We all wanted to attend and couldn't arrive at who would be denied. So, against our security's better judgment, here we are!"

"We agreed to make this brief," noted the second, "which is why we are first in line."

"We are thrilled that you two are together and grateful that you are back safely, Lugh," offered the third.

After the other six had expressed congratulations, their security immediately transported them to a secure location.

Santa, Mrs. Claus, Navva, Teeny Tiny Elf, Merlin, and Eliza hung back, allowing the guests to greet the couple. Merlin slid his arm around Eliza and whispered in her ear, "What an ending to your leprechaun book!"

Before she could reply, Bobby inserted, "My bringing Eliza and Lugh into these woods certainly has made this community interesting!"

Eliza chuckled. "That's true, Uncle Bobby."

Santa noticed an ugly scowl on Navva's face directed at Merlin. Did Navva have a problem with Merlin embracing Eliza? What was that?

Surveying the crowd, Santa noted that the who's who not only of the leprechaun community but all the elemental communities were in attendance. Spotting the ruling Royal Elves, he had an inkling Fiona's guest list had expanded beyond her control. Lugh's leadership was respected and appreciated throughout the elemental community.

Abruptly they were surrounded by Lugh's family. Aiden sidled up to Teeny Tiny Elf, Caoimhe embraced

Mrs. Claus, and Niamh grabbed Eliza's hand. "I want to introduce you to Lugh and my parents." Caoimhe began gesturing to each as she introduced. "This is our mother Aisling and our father Cormac."

"What a wonderful family you have!" Mrs. Claus enthused. "We are delighted to meet you."

"Yes," Santa agreed. "I echo my wife's greeting. Beside me are our daughter Eliza, her friend Navva, our long-time friend Merlin, and the special member of our family, Teeny Tiny Elf."

"We have heard a great deal about all of you," Lugh's mother replied. "We are honored to meet you."

Lugh's father shook his head. "We never dreamed our boy would associate with great wizards. He has lifted our clan to a new height."

"We love him dearly," Eliza responded, "and appreciate all he is doing to help elementals, humans, and the planet. He is an impressive leader."

"We met your grandfather Fitzsimmons," Santa offered. "He helped us locate a planet to which his twin brother had moved. Lugh looks just like him. "

"Fiona mentioned that—"

They were interrupted by a very excited Penelope and Designer. "What did you think of Fiona's dress? We designed it!" Penelope gushed.

"Beautiful!" Mrs. Claus replied.

"She gave us permission to use the design in our line," Designer added.

"Are you creating a line of wedding dresses?" Eliza wondered.

"A very limited one," Penelope noted. "Mine will be in it, too."

"Does J know that?" Eliza queried.

"Not yet," Designer confirmed.

"Dad!" Teeny Tiny Elf screamed. Spotting Malcolm stopping beside Santa, Teeny Tiny Elf dropped Aiden's hand and flew through the air to his dad. "What are you doing here?"

"I came to see the girls' creation and congratulate the couple," Malcolm explained. "What a crowd!"

Santa chuckled. "I think it's much larger than Fiona expected."

Malcolm craned his neck, searching. "Where's Mrs. Claus?"

"She left to check if Fiona needed more food," Santa noted. "I'm sure elves will be arriving with more any minute."

He was right. The guest list had ballooned, and Fiona was running low on food. Mrs. Claus gave the elves at the North Pole instructions on what to bring and asked that they do so quickly. When they arrived, she oversaw the placement of their creations. Then she returned to her family. "Just as you suspected, Dear, Fiona has a lot more guests than she invited," she announced.

The celebration filled the entire day. Around noon Oisin and several musicians began to play, which revitalized everyone by dancing to lively tunes. Late in the day, Eliza, Mrs. Claus, Santa, Navva, Merlin, Teeny Tiny Elf, and many neighbors helped clean up. When they finished, Eliza asked, "As the day has progressed, I have thought of additional questions I have about leprechauns. Would all of you come to my house for lunch tomorrow so that we can discuss them?" She paused. "Do you think I am proper asking Lugh and Fiona to join us?"

"You might be doing Lugh a favor," Mrs. Claus noted. "With your request Fiona may take tomorrow off. I'm sure he would appreciate her staying home."

Santa nodded. "Good point, Dear."

Encouraged by their approval, Eliza approached the couple. Lugh could not wipe the smile off his face. Eliza had not seen him this happy. Embracing first him and then Fiona, she congratulated, "What a wonderful day! I cannot find enough superlatives to express my happiness for you."

The rest of her group had followed and conveyed their compliments with hugs and words. Fiona breathed deeply. "Thank you so much, Mrs. Claus, for saving me with more food! I did not realize Lugh's popularity." She smiled at him. "Now I know."

Mrs. Claus smiled, too. "You are welcome. Santa was noting the crowd, which prompted me to check on the food. We were glad to be of help."

"Merlin commented that your hand-fasting is a wonderful addition to the book on leprechauns. May I include it?" Eliza requested.

In unison, the couple nodded. "We would be honored," Lugh voiced.

Eliza hesitated. "While enjoying the festivities today, I have come up with a few more questions about leprechauns. Would you come to my place for lunch tomorrow so that I may ask them of you? I've also invited Mother, Dad, Merlin, Navva, and Teeny Tiny Elf."

Lugh immediately replied, "We will be there." Looking at his wife, he repeated Mrs. Claus's statement, "I appreciate your invitation. The time is not too early so we can sleep in and lunch will keep Fiona home. I'd like to have at least one full day with her before she goes to work." He grinned at Santa. "We'll have to get her moved."

"I've already done that," Fiona volunteered.

"You have?!" Lugh cried, shocked.

"I meant what I stated to Eliza. From now on, I want to know if you are home or not. I'm not hearing it second hand. So, I moved in." She smiled slyly. "I figured that made hand-fasting a certainty."

By that time, everyone was laughing. "Come about 11:30," Eliza finalized.

Chapter 9

The following morning about ten, on impulse Eliza called J. "Do you have a few minutes?"

"Right now?"

"Yes. I have items you will find fascinating."

Ever since Eliza had introduced Penelope and Designer's creations to J, her interest was always piqued when Eliza called. "I have twenty minutes. Will that work?"

"See you shortly," Eliza finished.

A couple minutes later J's assistant announced Eliza. As she stepped into J's office, J remarked, "Did you transport in?"

Eliza grinned. "I did. I am very excited."

Setting down two bulging bags, Eliza unzipped the first one and placed five coils of thread on J's desk. As J picked one up, Eliza opened the second bag and unloaded four more coils. J had lifted one to her nose. "This smells divine! What is it?"

"The fragrance of the plant material from which it was made. Isn't it heavenly?" Eliza gushed.

Mesmerized by the scents, J was sniffing the other eight. Turning each completely around, she visually inspected the coils. "How distinctive!" she exclaimed. "What elemental makes these?"

"Fiona."

"The leprechaun who creates the fabrics for Penelope and Designer's line?"

"Yes. Their second line which infused scents into the fabrics prompted Fiona to add aromas to her threads, too. I thought you might have ideas of how to market them."

"I have very good friends who are extremely influential in the stitchery business. They would go wild over these," J responded. "May I keep them?"

"With my compliments," Eliza consented. "Get back to me with your suggestions." She paused. "I'll leave you my bags. By the way, Penelope and Designer are creating a short line of wedding dresses. Fiona and Lugh were married yesterday, and hers will be a part of the line as will Penelope's. Fiona's was breath-taking."

"Will yours be in the line, too?"

Eliza stared, speechless, at J for what seemed a long time to both. Finally, she voiced, "I don't have any wedding plans."

J attempted to lighten the moment. "C'mon, Handsome hasn't proposed yet?"

Eliza's solar plexus tightened, and she had a very bad feeling. Unable to express herself in words, she shook her head and muttered, "No."

Changing the subject, J stood and held out her hand. "Thanks for dropping by with these threads and giving me the update on Penelope and Designer. I will let you know what I find out."

Mustering a weak smile, Eliza shook J's hand and transported home. She immediately sank into a chair near the kitchen table. Dusty and Chance rushed up to her. Bending her head between them and hugging them close, she cried, "Something's wrong with Navva, Babies. Something's very wrong."

After a bit, she gave each of them a kiss, stood, and headed to the refrigerator. Taking a deep breath, she murmured, "I'd better get lunch ready."

Her disquiet regarding Navva was so great that upon arrival Santa and Mrs. Claus immediately detected her upset. What was that about? They wondered. Not wanting to broach the subject at that time, they tucked it away.

Navva noticed Eliza's red-rimmed eyes. "What's wrong?"

He couldn't read her look. "Nothing," she mumbled.

Still basking in the glow of their prior day's hand-fasting, Lugh and Fiona seemed to have permanent smiles on their faces.

Turning to Fiona, Eliza described her meeting with J. "I left the coils with her," Eliza finished. "I hope that was okay with you."

"Sure. I'm thrilled over her enthusiasm and yours. Thank you for showing them to her so quickly."

Lugh chuckled. "You'll learn that Eliza is never slow about anything. As Santa will attest, expect results and fast when you give her something."

Santa nodded. "That's for sure."

"Nona is her most recent example," Merlin agreed.

"She picked that up from me," Teeny Tiny Elf stated confidently.

After they ate and cleared the dishes off the table, Eliza

explained their purpose, indicating Lugh, Fiona, Merlin, and her parents. "Sean offered to answer more questions if I had them, but I wanted to try you guys first. While I thoroughly enjoyed meeting Sean, I thought asking the five of you would yield the same results but more quickly and without Sean's dramatic flair."

"He certainly added color to the interview and the book," Mrs. Claus remarked.

Lugh laughed. "I'm certain of that, which is one of the reasons I included him."

His comment caused Eliza to brighten. "You were right." Glancing down at her questions, she began, "He mentioned how leprechauns make mead, which I managed to hear despite Dad's interruption. He also referenced leprechauns pulling out the essence of drinks at a pub. Do leprechauns have a problem with alcoholism?"

"What an excellent question!" Fiona praised.

All five nodded. "We do," Lugh stated. "In fact we have a propensity for addiction not just to alcohol but in general. We also grapple with overindulgence in gambling."

"How does your community handle it?" Eliza wondered.

"Often leprechauns are in cities when they get caught

up in addictions. We have found the best solution is to send them back to their roots in the country," Lugh replied.

"Where there is less mead or gambling?"

"Where the leprechaun is forced to work with his hands, often at a craft. He also has closer oversight by relatives and friends. Both help steer the addict back on track," Lugh clarified.

"Too bad humans don't try that solution," Navva voiced.

"Leprechaun families keep better tabs on their kin than humans," Fiona responded, "which doesn't mean they are always successful, but they do address the problem."

"Why do leprechauns love honey?" Eliza asked.

Lugh grinned. "We consider bees our friends." He paused. "That feeling is prevalent in our community and goes way back. I don't know its origin." He looked at Mrs. Claus. "Do you?"

She shook her head. "I don't. Perhaps you will find out some other way, Eliza."

"I have a question of you, Mother," Eliza noted. "The leprechauns I have met on Earth get their nourishment from the essence of certain foods. Those on Nona were imbibing what you put in the water. I noticed you increasingly added more plant material to your concoction.

Do leprechauns receive sustenance from plants?"

"Yes, Dear, as well as the sun and even the air," Mrs. Claus confirmed.

"That's why Lugh likes to get a tan," spouted Teeny Tiny Elf.

Everyone laughed.

"Here's one for you, Dad. When we visited Flynn, I had the distinct impression he was well-read, but I have learned leprechauns do not have a written language. How does he bridge the language barrier of various human cultures?"

In unison, Santa and Lugh exclaimed, "Pictures!" Santa smiled and continued, "You discovered on Nona how much leprechauns communicate in holograms. That ability transcends language, making them easily understand what others' are conveying and vice versa, whatever the language, either written or oral."

"I was impressed that Caoimhe and Conor are teaching their children to read," Eliza directed at Lugh.

"They are forward-looking to a future where leprechauns and humans will communicate directly and know that, like you, humans will be impressed if leprechauns can read."

"That's true," Santa concurred.

"You were quite concerned that I received a well-rounded view of leprechauns, Lugh," Eliza noted. "You and Rosy did an excellent job making certain I did. Do you want to know that a particular subject – or two – was covered? If so, which ones?"

Nodding, Lugh thanked her. "I appreciate your checking with me on this. I intended to ask you before you completed the book. I have two. First, leprechauns are very emotional, which I believe you learned. Did you internalize the effect humans have on leprechauns?"

Eliza was perplexed and showed it. "No."

Lugh breathed deeply. "The goblin book explained how anger can blind humans to the truth." Indicating everyone around the table, he added, "We all understand the streak of anger permeating the human psyche these days. Humans do not realize that their thoughts and feelings affect the material world. Anger is a prominent example. Leprechauns and all elementals experience the results of humans' thoughts and feelings on the physical world, but we cannot do anything to change that. Only humans can."

Eliza was quiet, processing what Lugh had revealed. "So you want humans to realize the impact their thoughts and feelings are having on more than their existence?"

"Exactly."

"That's sobering," Navva stated.

"It is," Eliza agreed.

Merlin found his opening. "Did you address why leprechauns have an affinity for the color green?"

Eliza thought and then glanced around the table, ending at Lugh. "I don't think so. Was that on your list?"

He shook his head. "Why do we, Merlin?"

"Green symbolizes nature, represents the heart chakra, and is the color of balance. Leprechauns' emotional nature has a strong tie with harmony, which is why you embrace laughter, an equalizer that lifts, changes, and adjusts a mood, especially a negative one. Your laughter makes an impact with humans, helping them balance," Merlin explained. "Your propensity toward harmony naturally draws you to the color green."

Sensing that Eliza had absorbed that information, Lugh proceeded. "Thank you, Merlin. Your assessment leads right into my second concern. Did you discuss craic?"

"I've not heard that concept," Eliza replied.

Acknowledging Mrs. Claus, he explained, "Your mother was correct about the importance of sunlight and air as nutrition for leprechauns. Craic is as much nourishment for us as physical food."

Sitting on the edge of her seat, Eliza was intrigued. "What is craic?"

Santa started chuckling. Lugh glanced at him as if to say, 'Quiet!' "Craic is laughing, singing, dancing, doing anything that we consider fun. Leprechauns are the embodiment of fun, even laughing at ourselves for enjoyment. During the potato famine, we did not have much craic, and we suffered as much or more from the lack of craic as we did the lack of food. We thrive on craic."

"When we interviewed fairies I began to wonder if I was part fairy. Now I think I must be part leprechaun," Teeny Tiny Elf commented. "I love craic!"

"You never mentioned that," Eliza noted.

"I just learned about it," Teeny Tiny Elf rebutted. "How could I tell you what I didn't know?"

Feeling much better from the craic swirling around her kitchen, Eliza tickled Teeny Tiny Elf. "Yes, you are full of craic!"

"Maybe that's what's missing with humans," Navva speculated, "to recognize they need craic!"

For the first time that day, Eliza smiled at him. "Thanks! I'll put that in the book."

"Thank you, Eliza," Lugh complimented, "for making me feel a part of this book." He looked at his good friend

Santa. "Although I thank you for making certain all of the interviews Rosy and I had scheduled happened, I am sorry I missed them." He smiled slyly at Fiona. "I'm particularly sorry I missed your meeting Fiona, Eliza. I had been relishing that interaction. I understand you became speechless. A telling of that is just not enough."

"Why don't you and Fiona go back in time and view it?" Eliza queried.

Lugh's eyes widened. "That's a great idea! How about going there this afternoon, Fiona?"

Laughing, Fiona acquiesced, "Sure, Dear."

"Before you leave, I have one more question," Eliza stated. "Lucky numbers were mentioned at least twice in the interviews. What numbers are lucky?"

Lugh turned to Santa. "That one's yours." He paused. "And that's your daughter."

Santa rubbed his forehead. "I knew I wasn't going to escape this one." Materializing a book entitled *The Life You Were Born to Live*, he handed it to Eliza. "Start by reading this book. After that, we'll discuss numbers in depth."

Acting like she had just received a present she didn't expect, Eliza handled the book delicately. "Thanks, Dad. I will begin today."

Chapter 10

Nanna and Grandfather were re-hanging a cabinet door in the kitchen that had come loose. While Nanna held the door in place, Grandfather was on his knees tightening the screws through the hinge. Setting down the tool, Grandfather released a sigh. "There! I think that's tight."

Nanna leaned against the counter. "I miss Navva."

Grandfather smiled. "I do, too. I sure wish he would come back once in a while to help us out."

"He's having too much fun with Eliza and the excitement at the North Pole," Nanna noted.

Suddenly, Rebel leaped up, ran to the door, and scratched at it vigorously. "What is it, Boy?" Nanna wondered.

"Let him out. Something's out there," Grandfather urged.

Nanna opened the door, and they both watched him dash down the walkway to the Healing Place. Of one mind and without saying a word, they followed, curious. When they caught up with him, he was sitting in front of the entrance, patiently waiting for them to admit him. Slightly apprehensive, they looked at each other, wondering which one had the courage to crack open the door. Simultaneously they reached for the knob, turned it, and prepared to peek inside.

Despite their attempt to hold the door, Rebel pushed it open and ran over to the figure sitting on a chair with her back to them. She bent her head, gave Rebel a kiss, and softly whispered, "Hi, Boy, how are you?"

"Eliza!" Grandfather and Nanna shrieked in unison. "You are a welcome surprise!"

Rather than her normal exuberant response, Eliza remained seated and quiet. They walked around to face her. Her eyes red from crying and her cheeks still wet with tears, she managed a weak smile. "We had so many happy days here. I hoped that sitting here a bit would give me clarity." She shook her head. "It hasn't."

Both pulled a chair in front of her and sat down. "What's wrong?" Nanna asked.

"I don't know." Her voice cracked.

"Is something wrong with Navva?" Grandfather wondered, picking up her reference to happy days and assuming that indicated Navva.

"I think so."

Trying a different tactic, Grandfather offered, "Why do you say that?"

"His actions." She paused. Her dam of tears broke, and she sobbed. When she could talk again, she began, "I feel something is very wrong. The actions I'm about to tell you may sound relatively normal, but I feel they are not. You probably heard from Mother about my getting caught by the Disturbance and our work with the Nona."

"We did," Nanna acknowledged.

"Well, as we searched for Lugh and his crew, Navva exhibited extreme fear for my safety despite that I was with Dad–"

"That seems normal–" Nanna interrupted.

Grandfather placed his hand on hers and squeezed, physically suggesting she restrain her insertions.

Eliza looked from him to her. "When I returned from Nona the first time, he grabbed onto me and wouldn't let go. I finally gave him a second hug and another loving kiss to loosen his grip. He appeared desperate to keep me close to him."

Both remained silent, waiting for her to finish. They instinctively knew she had held the worst for last.

"Even though both of the actions I have described went over the top, you're right. They could understandably be ascribed to concern for me. Add what I'm about to tell you into the mix, however, and the situation becomes less easy to shrug off. Whenever Merlin stands close to me or embraces me in any way, Navva appears very irritated. If his eyes could shoot darts, Merlin's back would be pelted with them."

"Have you mentioned this to Navva?" Grandfather questioned.

Eliza shook her head. "No. I'm not certain he consciously acknowledges his actions. I doubt that he realizes I have noticed. When we were immersed in the Disturbance and Nona, I didn't allow my consciousness to acknowledge his behavior. Once we were past the crisis, his actions poured into the front of my mind, as if they had been waiting for the opportunity." She hesitated. "I cannot shake the feeling something is very wrong with him." Her voice dropped to a whisper. "I have a premonition I will be hurt by it in some way."

Taking another tactic, Grandfather wondered, "Have you talked to your parents about this?"

"Not yet. I will." She searched their eyes. "Truly, I came here not to involve you two but to seek relief from the tension building up within me."

"We appreciate your sharing with us," Nanna comforted.

Eliza placed her hands on top of Grandfather and Nanna's intertwined ones. "Whatever happens, please promise me you will help Navva. Don't be diverted by any action he has taken against me, Mother, or Dad. He needs your objectivity and love."

They were absorbing the gravity of the situation through Eliza's eyes.

"Do not tell him I was here or that I asked you to help him."

"What about his parents?" Nanna queried. "Can't they help him?"

"As we loaded the Disturbance to go back to Nona, Maria, uninvited, accompanied Scott and Violet to the beach. She screamed at Navva that he was in over his head; he should not go with us. He was not our caliber of wizard. He would be killed."

"Oh, dear," Grandfather sighed.

"I know Maria feels guilty that she left Navva with Teacher to be horribly treated. He is trying to be civil to her and embarrassed at her comments," Eliza explained.

"What does she say to you?" Nanna wondered.

"Nothing. She hasn't thanked me or even acknowledged my part in saving her, Justine, and Ilya. I seem to be invisible to her. She ignores me." Her hands squeezed theirs in gratitude. She looked into Nanna's eyes. "You say we're the perfect match. You may be right. I'm not certain that means we can be together." Her voice broke up. Managing to choke back her sobs, she finished, "Whatever happens, I want the best for him and that means he needs help."

Eliza stood. "I'd better go."

"Would you like some tea and cookies first?" Nanna offered.

"I have a Project Committee meeting tomorrow, and I want to review the manuscript for the leprechaun book one more time before we meet."

"Is it ready to go to press?" Grandfather wondered.

"With the Project Committee's approval, yes, it is."

Giving each of them a tight hug, Eliza disappeared home. Her sadness hung in the room. Nanna faced Grandfather. "What do you think?"

He seemed to have acquired Eliza's concern. "I think Eliza's right. Something is very wrong with Navva." He halted, thinking. "I hope her premonition is incorrect, and she doesn't get hurt, period."

They strolled in silence back to the house. As they neared, Grandfather had an epiphany. "I'm contacting Santa. He needs to know about this immediately."

Nanna smiled ruefully. "You're not waiting for Eliza to tell him like you did with the incidents here?"

"Exactly."

Santa, Nanna and I want to see you. Please come to our place as soon as possible.

The message had barely left Grandfather when Santa appeared in their circle. "Good Morning! How are you two doing?"

"We're fine. Let's sit down inside at the kitchen table," Nanna suggested. "I'll make some tea. Yesterday I baked a batch of your favorite cookies."

Santa kissed her on the cheek. "While I'm sure that's not why you summoned me, you certainly do know how to get my cooperation."

As she heated water for tea and set the cookies on the table, Grandfather opened the conversation. "We just had a visitor."

"Someone I know?" Santa wondered.

"Your daughter."

With a cookie halfway to his mouth, Santa halted. His eyes narrowed. "Where did you find her?"

"In the Healing Place. Rebel alerted us to her presence."

"She didn't contact you to let you know she was coming?"

They both shook their heads. "No," Grandfather replied.

"Where they had good times," Santa mumbled, seemingly to himself. He glanced from Grandfather to Nanna. "What did she say?"

Grandfather repeated the conversation word for word. When he finished, Santa breathed deeply. Again, as if to himself he mumbled, "So she has noticed." To Grandfather and Nanna, he voiced, "She's right. I've witnessed his actions, too. Every incident she mentioned has gotten my attention, and I have become increasingly concerned."

He paused, understanding one of the reasons Grandfather had summoned him. Addressing Grandfather specifically, Santa added, "She's not intentionally keeping this from her mother and me. We had an intense focus on helping those on Nona and are still processing that experience. Mrs. Claus and the elves at the Grounding Grounds are busy producing sustenance for every being on Nona. They are constantly adjusting the concoction to increase its nourishment." He breathed deeply. "I hadn't been certain Eliza had noticed his actions and am relieved to know she had. With our ardent effort on Nona, I'm not surprised she described Navva's actions as being in the back of her mind. Saving those beings and their children occupied the front of all our minds."

"How many are you feeding?" Nanna asked.

"Eighty-six adults and three hundred children," Santa replied.

Nanna and Grandfather gasped. "While that's a big number to feed," Grandfather noted, "it's a small number of residents for the entire planet. Is that all?"

"All who are alive," Santa responded. "We released an unbelievable number who had died."

Absorbing the tragic situation, the three sat in silence for a bit.

Nanna returned to Naava. "What do you think is happening with Navva?"

"I'm not certain."

"Do you have suspicions?" Grandfather prodded.

"Um hum," Santa replied. "He is exhibiting jealousy – at least that is part of it. I speculate Pan's nearness, however brief, to Eliza as a baby may have left an imprint which draws that out."

Grandfather mulled over Santa's theory. He slowly nodded. "Your postulation makes sense, particularly in light of their strong attraction and that they are both of an age to have children." He paused. "Any others?"

Santa shook his head. "No specific ones. However, I am certain there is more behind his actions than one simple problem. I sense he has an intense web of emotions tangled in his psyche."

"What do we do about it?" Nanna questioned anxiously. "Eliza has a premonition she will be hurt. How do we prevent that?"

"Keep her on the alert," Santa replied. "Navva must recognize he needs help and seek it out. I agree with my daughter. Neither she, her mother, or I are able to help him." He acknowledged them both. "She's right that you two could. Wait for him to ask, though."

"We will," Grandfather assured him. "Would you please update us on any significant happenings with him?"

"Certainly. The Project Committee's next focus is on tree devas. I wonder if Mittka will show up," Santa noted.

"Mittka!" Nanna shrieked. "Really?!"

"His presence fits the situation," Santa noted.

"You're right, he would. Hmm…" Grandfather concurred.

That evening Santa filled Mrs. Claus in on his visit. "You've answered our question about her noticing Navva's actions," she noted when he finished.

"I'm concerned about her premonition. She has a record of her foresights happening."

"What can we do?"

"Be more intent than ever watching and noting everything she and Navva say and do. This is a very tricky situation in which to protect her," Santa cautioned.

Mrs. Claus released a shaky breath. "I know, Dear. I know."

Chapter 11

Santa and Navva arrived early to the Project Committee meeting. Santa immediately enveloped his daughter in a tight embrace. Sending her calming energy, he attempted to alleviate her tension. He couldn't. She detected his effort and leaned against her favorite place, his shoulder, in order to draw in his energy. That didn't work, either. She felt isolated in her premonitory angst. He read her non-response. *Thanks for trying, Dad. I love you.*

Pulling away from him, Eliza pasted a bright smile on her face and turned to Navva. "Good Morning, Navva!" she expressed followed by a hesitant loving kiss.

Navva noticed her hesitancy, however brief, and flashed a perplexed look. "Are you okay?"

"I'm a little tired from reviewing the book several times

yesterday, but otherwise I'm fine," she replied, trying to cover what he had discerned.

Lugh materialized, interrupting their exchange. He was smiling broadly.

Eliza laughed. "Ever since your hand-fast, you constantly wear a smile. I think Fiona's presence agrees with you."

"If I would have known how wonderful I feel having her around, I would have insisted we live together long before you arrived," Lugh admitted. "She is a ray of sunshine in my life."

"I feel the same about Eliza," Navva echoed.

Lugh glimpsed the look of uncertainty that crossed Eliza's face. What was that about? He wondered.

He was distracted by the appearance of the rest of the committee, Patrick, Robin, Estel, Oakley, Rocky, and finally Booger. The last to arrive, Rosy hurriedly slid open the sunroom door, pushed past the others, and leaped into her seat. As everyone else settled into their chairs, Eliza set refreshments on the table.

Rosy could hardly contain her excitement. Politely restraining herself, she waited impatiently for Lugh to start the meeting. Perceiving her eagerness, Lugh deliberately dragged out his opening. "Did you all receive a copy of the leprechaun book?"

Everyone nodded. Some murmured, "I did."

"Have you all had a chance to absorb it?" Lugh further delayed.

"Stop it!" Rosy hollered. "I recognize your sense of humor responding to my enthusiasm."

Lugh feigned astonishment. "What?! I'm just checking that everyone has the manuscript and has reviewed it before we begin our discussion. I wouldn't want to be a spoiler."

"Right! I am a leprechaun, remember? I instantly spot leprechaun humor, which is exactly what you are employing," Rosy shot back.

Santa started chuckling. Eliza and then Navva joined him. Within a few seconds everyone except Rosy was laughing. Between chuckles, Lugh managed to eek out, "What do you think of the book, Rosy?"

Holding up the manuscript, she turned to Eliza. "This is by far the most accurate book on leprechauns ever written. I cannot give you enough compliments or express my excitement about it."

"I think I just received a great deal of both," Eliza replied between her bouts of laughter.

"I hope every leprechaun gets access to it," Rosy emphasized. "I want them to appreciate who they are and that humans may now have a clear picture, too."

"Rosy and Lugh, you made excellent choices of who to have Eliza interview. I didn't know leprechauns had bankers. I was amazed at that and many other pieces of information in the book," Estel noted.

"You certainly made this book personal, Lugh," Oakley remarked, "not only by having Eliza interview your family and friends, but also with the inclusion of your hand-fast and leprechauns on Nona."

"Lugh has a more interesting life than me," Rocky volunteered. "No one would have wanted to read about my boring life." He paused, glancing at Eliza. "Even with your writing skills, Eliza, you would not have been able present something about me personally that anyone would want to read."

"I wouldn't have wanted to share my life like Lugh did," Booger confessed. "I'm too private."

"Every single one of Eliza's books has been excellent," Patrick pointed out, "but Rosy and Lugh, you set the bar higher for us."

"Yes," Robin agreed. "You did. Thank you both for continuing this group's excellence and raising it."

Santa had finally gotten his laughter under control. "I, too, compliment Rosy and Lugh. I have long wondered what would finally prompt Lugh to tie the knot with Fiona. The answer is a book!"

"I'm thankful we could help his distant relatives on Nona," Navva contributed. "We came at just the right time. Some of the leprechaun children were in bad shape."

Eliza nodded. "The leprechaun kids seemed to be worse off than the Nonas, right, Dad?"

"I agree," Santa concurred. "I was very surprised a couple of them made it."

"They survived due to the determination of everyone helping," Lugh clarified. "That effort was a life-saving example of cooperation."

"Across cultures and planets," Eliza added.

His harassment of Rosy finished, Lugh expressed gratitude. "Thank you, Rosy, for pushing the interviews despite the disappearance of me and my crew. I understand your hesitation about even mentioning our having scheduled the interviews, but we are glad you did. After all, my crew and I just took a long nap!"

"If I have all of your approvals, I will lay out the book and get it to the printer," Eliza stated.

"Do we all approve?" Lugh asked.

"Absolutely!"

"Sure!"

"Why wouldn't we?"

"We're all in agreement to go to press," Lugh

summarized. Then he turned to Patrick and Robin. "You two are up next! Have you planned how you want to do this?"

"We have had several discussions on the topic," Robin replied. Looking at Estel and Oakley, he continued, "You two did an excellent introduction to trees, how they came to be on Earth, and some of their current challenges."

"That's right," added Patrick. "We do not feel the need to duplicate your efforts which were from the elves' understanding. We want to present our story through the trees' perspective."

"Similar to how the tree in the petrified forest took me back in time to when he was alive?" Eliza inserted.

"Exactly," Robin affirmed. "While all beings are important, trees have a unique function that touches all beings on this planet, whatever their dimension. First we plan to present more in depth information on trees so that everyone appreciates them fully."

Patrick picked up the thread. "Then we will explain tree consciousness, including tree devas, and finally devas, wherever they reside."

"We hope," expounded Robin, "our revealing devas will prompt this committee to expand our efforts beyond elementals to other beings on this planet—"

"Who humans need to understand," Patrick finalized.

"With these books we have piqued humans' interest," Robin commented. "Let's use this connection to tell about more."

"Leave it to a deva to open the door beyond," Santa remarked.

"How do you intend to do this?" Eliza wondered.

"We know you can communicate with trees," Patrick noted.

"I love to talk to trees!" Eliza agreed.

"We think that is amazing," Robin praised. "We want to use your ability to have you receive the information about their lives directly from the trees."

"We will take you around the planet for you to learn from trees and pass along in the book what you discover," Patrick detailed.

"Then we'll tell you about us," Robin continued. "Similar to Lugh, we will include our lives and experiences."

"We thought our examples would be the best approach," Patrick explained, "although we may include some friends. We haven't decided yet."

His mention of friends made the hair on the back of Santa's neck rise. About to ask "which friends," Santa received his answer.

A figure appeared behind Eliza's chair, rolled it out, and raised her up. She didn't have a chance to react as he wrapped his arms around her, drew her close to his chest, and pressed his lips over hers. Arching her back, he engaged her in a long, loving kiss. Captivated, she returned his embrace and kiss for way too long from Navva's perspective. As he straightened them both, he pulled away slightly and smiled into her eyes. "I've been anticipating that. You didn't disappoint."

She was staring at the most handsome man ever imagined. He exuded charm, grace, and attraction. He appeared to be the epitome of the perfect male. His energy enticed her to want another kiss and embrace. Brought back to reality, she resisted the impulse, knowing Navva was watching.

His arm encircling her waist, he turned toward Santa. "Hello, Mittka," Santa welcomed, feeling Navva's jealousy rise sharply.

Chapter 12

Suddenly, Mrs. Claus and Teeny Tiny Elf appeared with lunch. Intent on depositing the bundle overflowing in her arms, without looking around Mrs. Claus stepped over to the counter, carefully unloading her creations. As she released the last one, arms grabbed her from the back, swung her around, drew her close, and gave her a long, loving kiss. Much like Eliza, she enjoyed the experience, returning the kiss and the embrace. Mittka pulled back and smiled into her eyes. "I've missed you."

She laughed. "Yes, Mittka, no one kisses as enticingly as you."

Appalled, Navva gasped. Eliza's eyes widened in shock. Teeny Tiny Elf looked at Santa and voiced their concerns. "Santa, are you okay with Mrs. Claus kissing him?"

Santa echoed Mrs. Claus's laughter. "Why shouldn't I be?"

Teeny Tiny Elf didn't know what to say. "I thought married wizards only kissed each other."

Mrs. Claus picked up Teeny Tiny Elf and handed him to Mittka. "Teeny Tiny Elf, this is Mittka. Due to his touch with nature, elementals have the highest regard for him." She bent down and whispered, "He is the best kisser a female will ever meet."

"Would you like me to give you an example?" Mittka asked Teeny Tiny Elf.

He pointed. "Just on the cheek, please."

Channeling his loving energy into the kiss, Mittka pressed his lips to Teeny Tiny Elf's cheek. Teeny Tiny Elf felt a tingling through his body. "I felt your projection of love through my entire being. Wow! I understand what Mrs. Claus means." He reached up and gave Mittka a peck on the cheek. "That's not as powerful as yours, but that's the best I can do."

Mittka hugged him. "Thank you."

His question still not satisfied, Teeny Tiny Elf looked at Santa. "Doesn't that bother you, Santa?"

Santa shook his head. "Mittka is a perfect kisser. Why should I be upset if Mrs. Claus is enjoying perfection?"

Navva and Eliza could not think of a comment. Lugh welcomed, "We are honored to have you drop into our meeting, Mittka."

"Patrick and Robin invited me."

"Yes, Mittka has agreed to introduce Eliza to other devas," Patrick explained.

Mittka's eyes locked with Navva's. "Yes, I have. I'm looking forward to it."

Rosy was impressed. "Wow! To have a being of Mittka's status will help in our efforts. Please don't get me wrong, everyone, but he will raise our credibility among elementals substantially."

"I agree," Estel and Oakley chorused.

Ready to eat, Lugh wrapped up the meeting. "If you are finished, Patrick and Robin, this meeting is concluded, and we'll enjoy Mrs. Claus's lunch. Will you join us, Mittka? I'm sure Mrs. Claus has plenty."

Everyone agreed, including Mittka. Teeny Tiny Elf had hopped onto the counter to grab a dish to serve. "Would you like to help us serve, Mittka?"

"Of course," Mittka responded, picking up a couple of dishes and taking them to the table. He knew just which being received each.

As they ate, Mittka mentioned, "I understand the book you are about to release concerns leprechauns. Tell me about it."

Rosy and Lugh enthusiastically described the book with insertions here and there from all the other members of the committee. When they finished, Mittka remarked, "Sounds as good as the others. I'm looking forward to it."

Eliza's jaw dropped. "You have been reading these books?"

"Of course!" Mittka responded. "What's important to the elementals is important to me. Do you think all I do well is kiss?"

His response reminded her of a comment her dad had made about dropping off presents at Christmas being his only talent. She grinned at Santa. Reading her mind, he grinned back. "I'm certain that like Dad you are multitalented."

Mittka became very serious. "We are all intent on keeping this planet inhabitable. The Project Committee's work is a critical step in that direction." He looked around the table. "Thank you all for your contributions."

After everyone finished lunch, they went home, including Mittka. Eliza grabbed the dogs' leashes and offered, "Want to go for a walk, guys?"

Anxious to talk to her tree friend, she did not initiate her circular-energy-pattern-detector and didn't discern his presence until he spoke. "You're slipping in not running your energy-detector. At this time of your life, that's not wise."

Simultaneously, Eliza halted and jumped, yanking Dusty and Chance back toward her. "Mittka! You scared me."

"I meant to do so," he replied. "You are in a dangerous energy. Be alert and careful."

"What do you mean?"

He bent down, petting both dogs. "Hello Dusty and Chance. Nice to meet you." In response, their tails wagged rapidly.

"Your exposure to Pan as a newborn set up your current situation." He paused. "Let me back up and introduce myself as most elementals know me. I am the true Pan."

Eliza gasped. Instantly running her circular-energy-pattern-detector, she did not read Pan's essence. "You won't find his essence on me," Mittka stated.

Her head spun. "I am confused. Why would you claim to be that awful individual?"

"He used my identity. I existed long before him,"

Mittka explained. "Elementals strongly associate me with Nature, which is why they revere me. I love them deeply and am always here to help them." He smiled. "Due to humans associating Nature with spring, the birds and the bees, and consequently reproduction, my connection to Nature on this planet has given me an unparalleled attraction, particularly with females. You felt that today from my kiss and so did your mother."

"I am still trying to process her response to your kiss," Eliza admitted.

"That's not unusual. While my attraction is appreciated and enjoyed by women, men do not have the same reaction."

"Really?!" Eliza snidely responded.

He laughed. "I like you. You are a enchanting combination of your parents and more. I'm impressed."

"Thank you. Being associated with my parents is a high compliment to me."

Captivated by her eyes, his gaze shifted to her lips, and he gathered every bit of constraint to avoid kissing her again. Inwardly struggling, he resumed his story. "Men's response to me is a mixture of red emotional vibrations, including jealousy, anger, and inadequacy as Navva exhibited today."

"What does that have to do with the entity we call Pan?"

"He found the negative red vibrations powerful, latched onto them, and now embodies them. They are not my vibrations. They are the energies of those who dislike me."

"Why did he target Dad? Why not target you?"

"Because I would de-manifest him. Your dad will not."

"But my dad could? Are you more powerful than Dad?"

"Yes, your dad could. Your dad and I have never compared our power. Let's just say we are both very powerful."

"And the entity we call Pan attacks Dad because it knows Dad will not get rid of it?" Eliza surmised.

"Right. Your parents' embodiment of love, joy, and kindness is unparalleled." He drew a deep breath. "You may exceed theirs, which is difficult for me to imagine, but I detect you may have that in you."

"Did you stop calling yourself Pan because that entity pretended to be you?" Eliza wondered.

"Partly," he agreed, "and partly to brand myself with a new name that gave me the opportunity to reflect how I had grown to be more than a powerful nature deity."

"You stated my exposure to Pan's anger is affecting me now. Why?" Eliza questioned.

"You are of the age to have children. You are beautiful and alluring to men. Those three factors alone trigger the red vibration from him which remains around you."

"Can you de-manifest it from me?"

He did a double-take. "You are fast! No one has ever requested a de-manifestation from me that quickly." Another overwhelming desire to kiss her engulfed him. This time he gently pulled her to him, satisfying himself and Eliza with another long, loving kiss. As he leaned back from her with passion in his eyes, he revealed, "You are special. If I didn't know your parents, I'd compete with Navva for your affection."

Pecking a teasing kiss on his lips, her eyes twinkled. "I find you very attractive, too, but I am not interested in anything more than friendship."

"I understand. You want Navva," he returned. "That is why I cannot de-manifest the red vibration from you right now. I might chase away, hurt, or worse de-manifest Navva. That is too risky." He paused and looked at her intently. "You intuit more is wrong with Navva than jealousy."

Tears welled up in her eyes. "I do." She hesitated. "Can you fix him?"

"He must decide to fix himself." Mittka halted. "But you know that, too, don't you?"

Gently pressing him up against the tree behind him, Eliza initiated one more loving kiss, the longest of the three they had enjoyed. Barely removing her lips from his, Eliza searched his eyes. "I intend this third lucky kiss to seal our friendship forever." He responded by doubling the length of the kiss.

After drawing back and regaining his breath, he revealed, "You are taking my breath away. I don't know if anyone has ever affected me so strongly."

Her eyes twinkled. "Perhaps it's the red vibration."

He smiled, too. "Perhaps. Navva is one lucky guy." He glanced at her friend the tree. "Your friend is anxious to talk to you. I'll see you soon. Remember to use your energy-detector."

Before disappearing, he stepped up to the tree and had a few words. Flashing Eliza an enticing smile, he vanished.

"He's taken with you," her friend began.

"I like him, too," Eliza replied, "as a friend."

"You stirred more interest in him than he had anticipated."

Eliza chuckled. "He needs to be kept on his toes."

"He is a powerful ally."

"I perceived that," Eliza noted. She asked the question pressing on her psyche. "Is the fourth prophecy fulfilled?"

"Not yet."

"Really?!" Eliza was disappointed. "I thought our work with Nona and the leprechauns would accomplish that."

"No question those two factors were an important part of the prophecy, but the toughest part lies ahead." The tree paused and added, "Rosy is correct. Your book on leprechauns is about to make a huge impact on that elemental community. They will all walk a little taller after being exposed to it."

"That's gratifying." Eliza hesitated, wanting to phrase her next question just right. "Is Navva critical to the rest of this prophey's fulfillment? Does he need to heal in order for the fourth prophecy to be completed?"

The tree was silent.

Understanding the tree's silence signaled the end of their conversation, Eliza turned to the dogs. She sighed. "Let's go, guys."

"Mittka's caution was correct," the tree volunteered unexpectedly. "Pay attention to your energy-detector. You have dangerous energy around you which is attracting even more dangerous energy. Be careful not to get caught up in it."

The unusualness of the tree's reply had the desired impact on Eliza. She paid closer attention to her circular-energy-pattern-detector…for a while, anyway.

Chapter 13

Very apprehensive that Mittka might tag along on the interviews which Patrick and Robin had set up, Santa took an uncharacteristic action. To alleviate his angst, he arrived along with Mrs. Claus, Teeny Tiny Elf, and Navva to Eliza's the morning of the first one. His unease was immediately confirmed. Mittka had appeared earlier, and he and Eliza were sharing another loving kiss.

Instantly upset, Navva did not even offer to kiss Eliza.

An equal opportunity kisser, Mittka moved to Mrs. Claus, embraced her, and gave her one, too. When he pulled back, Teeny Tiny Elf hopped onto Mittka's arm, hugged him, and whispered into his ear, "I'll take one on the cheek, please."

Smiling, Mittka did as Teeny Tiny Elf asked. He grinned. "That was nice!" Turning to Navva, he added, "Try a kiss from Mittka, Navva. You'd like it."

Without giving Navva a chance to reply, Santa requested, "Could I talk to you outside, Mittka?"

When they reached the deck, Santa turned to Mittka. "What are you doing?"

"Patrick and Robin invited me along on these interviews so here I am."

Santa was exasperated. "I understand they invited you, but that is not the main reason you are here."

"I really like your daughter. We have established a firm friendship."

Santa's eyes narrowed. "Did you return after the meeting broke up?"

Mittka nodded. "We had a private tete-a-tete."

Suspicious, Santa interrogated, "Was that all?"

Mittka sighed like he had just relinquished his favorite thing. "Sadly, yes. If I didn't have so much respect for you and Mrs. Claus, I'd compete with Navva for her affection."

"Do you think you could?"

He stared blankly at Santa for a few seconds, thinking. "Actually, no, I don't. She knows what she wants and is determined enough to ignore me."

Santa smiled. "I'm glad to hear that assessment from you."

"Why?"

"I share your view. Your admission solidifies my confidence in her." Santa paused. "What about Navva?"

Mittka shrugged. "He's your concern, not mine. You know him. You understand what is going on with him."

Santa shook his head. "Not really." He breathed deeply. "I do not want to interrupt the interviews Patrick and Robin have set up. Even though both you and Eliza are enjoying your kisses, for Navva's sake don't make them so long."

"Do you think that will help?"

"I hope so." Santa's look of doubt belied his words.

When they returned to the kitchen, Patrick and Robin had arrived. "We are beginning close to home," Patrick revealed. "Santa, would you transport us to the coordinates I am sending you?"

"Certainly," Santa replied, doing so immediately.

They materialized beside a majestic oak. "We're a couple miles away from my place!" Eliza exclaimed. Glancing around, she became teary-eyed. "The tornado missed these…thankfully."

"We were sorry for the ones that went down in your woods," the oak noted.

Stretching her arm, Eliza stroked the tree's bark. "Thank you. I miss them every day."

Rousting herself out of her reverie, she asked Patrick and Robin her first question. "What is a tree deva?"

"A higher consciousness that hangs around trees," Robin replied.

"Do devas inhabit all trees?"

"No," Patrick returned. "As your dad taught you, everything has consciousness, so all trees are conscious. Devas are a more evolved consciousness. They do not inhabit every tree."

"Is that why you are more flexible to leave your trees and attend our meetings?"

"That's why you see us as a hologram and not a full blown tree," Robin agreed.

Teeny Tiny Elf started to chuckle. "The image of you picking up your roots and stumbling into Eliza's kitchen is funny."

"I'm glad you mentioned how you appear to us," Eliza concurred. "Many human readers may see you as doing what Teeny Tiny Elf just described."

Navva was caught up in the discussion. "Why do trees have devas? Other plants don't have devas. Why trees?"

For the first time that day, Eliza smiled at Navva. "Thank you. That's a good question."

Their eyes locked, and he felt they were back at The Healing Place where she had made him feel confident. No one else had done that to him.

"As Mittka will show you, Eliza," Patrick answered, "devas exist throughout nature on this planet. Their consciousness level is comparable to an angel. Elementals revere them in a similar fashion to how humans admire angels."

"And not just the elves," inserted Teeny Tiny Elf.

Mittka laughed. "You're right. All elementals, not just elves, hold devas in high regard."

"Devas oversee and channel a high vibration to those within their charge," Robin noted.

"The fairies taught me that angels create and oversee them. Do the angels oversee plants through the fairies?" Eliza wondered.

"Good call!" praised the oak. "They do."

Eliza's brow furrowed. "Why don't fairies tend trees?"

She felt laughter emanating from the oak, Patrick, and Robin. Mittka, Mrs. Claus, and Santa joined them in laughing out loud. The oak was the first to compose itself enough to answer. "Excuse us. The image of delightful fairies tending trees is humorous. We are too big and complex for fairy energy."

"Similar to gnats around humans?" Eliza commented.

"Exactly!" Robin agreed.

"Do devas inhabit certain species of trees?"

"We love oaks," Patrick remarked, "but we will reside in any tree."

"Why oaks?" Eliza questioned.

"They have always felt comfortable to us," Robin responded. "Perhaps it's because they drive their roots deep into the ground which makes them very sturdy–"

"Or their slow and steady growth," Patrick inserted. "We tree devas prefer that pace. We are not in a rush."

"Oaks live hundreds of years, giving us lots of time within their structure," the oak added. "Whatever the reason, oaks have been our choice, speaking for all three of us, anyway."

"Yes," Robin revealed, "Patrick and I both reside in oaks, too."

"Back to Navva's question," Eliza referenced. "Specific plants don't have their own devas. Fairies and angels overseeing them have that function. Why do trees have devas especially for them?"

"Because trees are unique," Robin quickly replied.

"How?"

"We have an important impact on this planet," the oak added. "We are an anchoring force."

"That's right," Patrick expounded. "We hold the surface of the planet together."

"The parts of the planet that are barren of trees have the most erosion," Navva noted.

"With no trees to catch the wind, it wreaks havoc on the ground," Robin concurred.

"Trees contribute to the establishment of soil," Patrick pointed out.

"And keep it healthy through replenishment," Mrs. Claus inserted.

"We enable propagation of many living organisms above ground, in the top soil, and deep in the subsoil," the oak explained.

"Basically, trees create a livable environment," Patrick concluded.

"Yes, without trees Earth would not be habitable," Robin piggybacked.

Eliza smiled at her dad. "That's why Dad plants hundreds every spring."

"We're very grateful for that effort," the oak noted. "We know the North Pole elves are excited to help. Thank you and please thank them from all the trees around the planet."

"Trees make a huge difference," Eliza stated. "I want

to communicate that in this book. I have a strong affection for trees and think they are not understood by humans. Will these interviews help me enlighten humans about trees?"

"Yes," enthusiastically replied the oak. "We will give you information about trees that most people do not know. We hope that will pique their interest to know more."

"And to treat trees with more respect," added Patrick.

"We'd like trees to be loved and appreciated for their contributions to making this environment livable, not because they are a source of lumber and firewood," expressed the oak.

"Thank you, Eliza, for your concern about trees. I think we are on the same wavelength regarding them. After this introduction, tomorrow we will delve into the cooperation between trees," Robin announced.

Eliza was amazed. "Cooperation? You've piqued my interest. I've never viewed trees as living cooperatively."

With the interview concluded, Santa transported them back to Eliza's. Mittka was the first to leave. "See all of you tomorrow," he noted as he disappeared.

Sliding his arm around Eliza, Navva whispered, "Thanks for the compliment today."

As she turned to him, smiling, he tentatively gave her a loving kiss. "You are welcome."

"See you tomorrow," Teeny Tiny Elf cried, waving to Eliza as they transported home.

Lying in bed that night, Mrs. Claus mentioned to Santa. "Watching Navva today, I was struck by his shaky confidence."

"Eliza bolsters him," Santa replied.

"I was surprised to note that. He seems very competent to me."

"He is," Santa agreed. "He doesn't think he is, though."

"Teacher's influence no doubt," Mrs. Claus concluded.

"No doubt," Santa echoed in agreement.

"When Eliza was gone, Navva tried to distract himself from worrying about her every second by spending time with Justine and Ilya. Unfortunately, that gave him more exposure to Maria," Mrs. Claus reflected. "Due to her guilt about leaving him with Teacher, she projects negative energy toward Navva."

"You're right. She is eroding his confidence." He changed the subject. "I'm very worried about Mittka's involvement in these excursions so I'm accompanying the group on each one for Navva's sake and Eliza's."

Sighing, she rested her head on Santa's shoulder. "Maybe they won't make it."

"Whether they do or not, I want Navva to be emotionally healthy for his sake. He needs our support to heal from Teacher's upbringing."

Chapter 14

Respecting Santa's request, the following morning Mittka shortened the length of his kiss with Eliza. That didn't seem to assuage Navva's upset. He had become so touchy about Mittka and Eliza that even Mittka standing near her drove up Navva's ire.

Mittka had barely finished kissing Mrs. Claus and Teeny Tiny Elf when Patrick and Robin arrived. "Good Morning, Patrick and Robin! Where are we off to today?" Eliza asked.

"A group of trees," Robin replied. "Santa, would you please transport us to the coordinates in my thoughts?"

"Will do," Santa returned.

They materialized in the middle of a beautiful group

of oaks. The trees appeared so perfectly shaped that Eliza felt she had been dropped into an exquisite sculpture. "Wow!" She exclaimed. "Are you ever gorgeous!"

"Thank you," acknowledged one. "We are honored to talk with you and provide information for your book."

"As mentioned yesterday, we want to address the social nature of trees," Patrick reminded them.

"You indicated they lived cooperatively." Walking up to the nearest in the group, she asked, "How do you do that?"

"We look out for each other," the tree responded.

"And help one another," the next one added.

Eliza picked up the thread. "Let's start with looking out. Give me examples of your doing that."

"If we sense danger from small invaders to large animals, we alert the trees to which we are connected."

"You are connected?" Eliza repeated.

"Yes. Our roots come together either by intertwining, the tips touching, or fungi networks creating a pathway between us."

"Seriously?!" Eliza exclaimed. "My impression was that your root connections were a bad thing because you can spread disease and pests through those corridors."

She felt the group of trees give the impression of a

laugh. "Humans tend to bring out the negative in everything. While that may happen, overall our connections are a very positive factor for all of us," noted a tree to her right.

One behind her offered, "We help each other through those attachments."

"How?" Eliza wondered.

"If one in our group is not doing well, we feed it what it needs to heal, whether that is sugar, nutrition, or water."

Aghast, Eliza cried. "You help each other heal? I didn't know that trees could heal at all. Healing each other floors me." She glanced at her parents. "Did you know that trees heal at all? Did you know they heal each other?!"

Mrs. Claus and Santa smiled. "Yes, Dear, we do know both," Mrs. Claus assured their daughter.

"Trees heal themselves, too," Santa expounded, "like you."

"They do?!" Eliza's shock continued. "I am learning a lot!"

Taking in the entire group, Eliza noted, "You remind me of the relationship I have with my best friend Kandarry. We heal each other."

"Just like your relationship with Kandarry, we, too, thrive when we are with friends. When we lose a friend, we are sad," the one in front of her explained.

"And somewhat helpless," another one added. "That friend's loss may cut us off from our other friends, thereby jeopardizing our health through lack of a network that heals us."

"Oh, my goodness," Eliza exclaimed. "I have a new perspective on how the loss of most trees in my woods from the tornado affected the few that remained."

"The ones that were isolated and not close to another tree at all were in grave danger of not surviving," informed one to Eliza's left.

She had an epiphany. "That's why the second and even third year after the tornado more died!"

"They hung on as long as they could, but, without their social network for support, they were doomed," another tree in front of her agreed.

"In addition to our root systems joining, we cooperate above ground, too. Our branches form a canopy which retains moisture, breaks the wind, and protects from heat and cold. Together we create an ecosystem that helps us thrive, live long lives, and enjoy existence through each other's company," explained a tree to her right.

Mittka entered the conversation. "The advantages to trees of forming a community are similar to those of humans. Alone, a human has more vulnerability. With others, a human increases longevity through protection, assistance, and shelter."

Momentarily forgetting his ire, Navva became caught up in Mittka's comparison. "That's fascinating, Mittka. Trees and humans experience the same challenges of physical existence and use the same solutions to address them. Hmm…"

Thrilled by Navva's reiteration and attention, Mittka, who was standing near Navva, grabbed him and planted a big kiss on his cheek. "Excellent expansion of my point!"

"Navva! You were kissed by Mittka!" Teeny Tiny Elf exclaimed. "How did it feel?"

His face crinkling as if he had touched something vile, Navva wiped off Mittka's kiss.

Ignoring their drama, Eliza noted, "That community creates a dependency–"

"Which makes each member valuable…another reason when one tree is not doing well the others help. Doing so is in all their best interests," pointed out the first tree.

"Look up," Robin instructed. "Notice how the edge of the branches of each tree do not infringe on the branches of the trees next to it? The trees are respectful of each other's space and deliberately hold back their spread to keep all trees near them strong."

Grasping the trees development of community, Eliza murmured, "They don't want to intrude on their friends' space because that might weaken their friends through loss of photosynthesis in their leaves. Interesting…"

"What happens if a tree in this situation dies from being cut down or ill health?" Navva questioned.

"We lose the benefit of that tree's branches," noted one of the trees who had not yet responded. "Sometimes we are able to continue to use its root system, though."

"A tree's root system can remain viable after the upper part of the tree is gone?" Eliza repeated. "Wow!"

"We do our best for all our sakes to keep it, and therefore our network of roots, going," confirmed another tree.

"The trees humans plant to harvest," Santa contributed, "like those for Christmas, usually don't have the opportunity to feel community because their root system connection is severed by the irregular cutting of those nearby. We receive tremendous joy from the ones we rescue when they experience cooperation for the first time in their forever locations."

Eliza's jaw dropped. "I didn't realize that!" She twirled around, taking in the entire group of magnificent oaks. "You have given me absolutely marvelous information. Thank you very much. Do you have any more?"

Patrick broke the silence. "They covered the subject well. We echo our thanks for their input."

"You are very welcome," they responded in unison.

"I am so glad to talk to you and hear your responses," Eliza finished.

"So are we," the first one replied. "Your ability is a big plus."

After everyone else thanked the trees and bid goodbye, Santa returned the visitors to Eliza's kitchen. Mittka offered, "Good interview Patrick, Robin, and Eliza." He smiled at Navva. "Thanks for your comments, too, Navva. See you in a couple days." He immediately disappeared.

"Yes, thank you all, especially Eliza and Navva, for an excellent interview," Patrick added.

"You covered all we had hoped and more," Robin concluded. "We will see you in two days."

They both disappeared amid good-byes from the remaining five.

In hopes of dispelling Navva's anger, Eliza stepped over to him, gave him a loving kiss, and echoed Mittka's remark. "Yes, thank you, Navva. You always have insightful observations." Sliding her arm around Navva's back, she turned to her parents and Teeny Tiny Elf. "For once I don't have any appointments this afternoon. I prepared a special lunch in advance, hoping to convince you four to stay. Would you, please?" As she asked, she turned to Navva, seeming to direct the invitation particularly to him.

Santa and Mrs. Claus waited for his response. Giving Eliza a smile, he replied, "That sounds good. Thank you."

"I think so, too," Teeny Tiny Elf chimed in. "How about you, Santa and Mrs. Claus?"

"We're both hungry," Mrs. Claus returned. "Would you like help?"

"Let's enjoy the nice day out on the deck," Eliza remarked. "I have a dish for each of you to carry. I'll bring the plates, tableware, and napkins."

They paraded out to the deck, each with a contribution toward lunch in hand. Settling into their favorite chairs, they savored the meal Eliza had made. Their conversation revolved around the morning's interview. For the first time since the Disturbance had appeared, Eliza and Navva chatted comfortably. Those were precious family moments which in a few days they all wished they could retrieve.

Chapter 15

The sound of a loud motor roaring up the driveway was followed by tires screeching to a halt at the garage.

"Were you expecting someone?" Mrs. Claus asked her daughter.

Eliza shook her head. "No." Turning to Teeny Tiny Elf, she advised, "In case it's a human, would you please go in the house?"

"I'll visit Eddie," he offered instead, leaping off the deck, zipping over to the flower bed, and switching dimensions as he moved.

They heard a car door slam. A voice slurred, "Pretty nice place. A little lacking in trees, though."

Eliza felt goosebumps surge up her back as the

footsteps thudded toward the deck. She looked apprehensively from her mother to Navva to her dad.

Santa gave her a quizzical look.

As the footsteps reached the deck, the figure rounded the corner and noticed four sitting at the table, their empty plates from lunch in front of them. "Eliza! You had a party and didn't invite me?! Imagine that!"

"Hello, Roger. What are you doing here?"

He stared at her angrily. "I finally found you! I have been searching ever since you disappeared."

Eliza sat quietly, struggling to determine how to handle the situation.

"Aren't you going to invite me to join you?"

"I didn't invite you to my house."

"At least you could introduce me." Stepping over to Mrs. Claus, he held out his hand. "I'm Roger."

Ignoring his hand, she replied, "Do you normally go to a home uninvited and not welcome?"

Bending down, Roger stuck his face a couple inches from Mrs. Claus's, blowing alcohol-laced breath on her. "You are a –"

"Roger!" Eliza screamed, "You will not talk to her that way!"

"Why not? By right, she's on my property. This place should be half mine."

Unable to contain himself, Navva cried, "What?!"

Moving away from Mrs. Claus, Roger stepped over to Navva. "Who are you? Her new beau? Give it up, Man. You can't have what is already taken." To punctuate his statement, Roger pounded Navva on the shoulder.

Navva began to rise, but Santa clapped a hand on Navva's arm in restraint.

Blogger, Santa telepathically communicated, *Would you please call Officer Griffin? Say you're Eliza's friend. Ask him to come to Eliza's immediately. She is being harassed by a guy.*

Sure, Santa.

Acknowledging Santa's holding back Navva, Roger prodded, "Smart move. He needs protection. I'd take care of him fast."

Santa's eyes narrowed.

Something about his look sent a warning chill through Roger. Gesturing to Santa and Mrs. Claus, Roger addressed Eliza, "Who are these individuals? Scammers out to take your money?" Indicating Navva, he added, "This guy probably thinks you're hot." Turning to Navva, Roger continued, "You're right; she is. You can't have her, though, she's mine."

They hadn't heard Officer Griffin arrive. He had deliberately driven in quietly to determine the situation.

When he spoke, Roger jumped. "Is this gentleman bothering you, Eliza?"

She nodded. "He is here uninvited. I would like him to leave."

"I'm Officer Griffin. What is your name, Sir?"

"Roger. I have a right to be here. Half this property is mine."

"How is that, Sir?"

"Eliza is my wife, and half of what she owns is mine."

Navva and Mrs. Claus simultaneously gasped.

"Do you have a marriage license, Sir?"

"No. She tore it up."

"I suggest you get a duplicate and present it to the court," Officer Griffin calmly stated. "Stay off this property. I do not want to receive another call that you are here. Next time I will arrest you for trespassing."

"These people are scamming her out of my money! You should be arresting them!"

Pointing first at Mrs. Claus and then Santa, Officer Griffin replied, "These are Eliza's parents."

Starting with a guffaw which broke out into a full blown vicious laugh, Roger finally got control of himself. "Her parents?! Her parents are dead! That's how she got all her money. They died in a car accident, and she made a bundle from their deaths because they died accidentally! Her parents! You've been hoodwinked, Man."

Officer Griffin turned to Eliza. "Are these your parents, Eliza?"

"These are my biological parents, Officer Griffin. The ones who died in the car accident were my adoptive parents," Eliza clarified.

"Are you married to this man, Eliza?" Officer Griffin continued.

"No."

"Have you ever been married to his man, Eliza?"

"No." She paused. "He wishes I had been."

Roger interrupted scornfully, "Your biological parents! Where did you find them? You never mentioned knowing your biological parents when we were together."

Although Eliza was sorely tempted to say they had never been together, she held herself in check, knowing the less she said the faster Officer Griffin would get Roger out of there.

"Walk ahead of me to your vehicle, Sir," Officer Griffin ordered. "Get into your vehicle and drive in front of me out of here. Do not return. I repeat, if I come back here because you have returned, I will arrest you."

Roger flashed a nasty glance at Eliza. "I'll be back for

you and your money. You can't take it away from me now that I've found you."

Officer Griffin addressed Eliza. "Call me if he comes back. Thank your friend for letting me know about this situation. I assume she stayed in the house."

Eliza nodded. "She did and I will. Thank you for coming quickly."

He smiled. "I'm here to serve." Turning to Mrs. Claus, Santa, and Navva, he ended, "Have a good day. Ma'm. Sir. Navva."

They remained quiet until they could no longer hear the two vehicles. Switching dimensions and rushing from the flower bed, Teeny Tiny Elf broke the silence. "Do you know that Roger, Eliza?"

"Unfortunately, I do," she replied.

"Did you date him?" Navva demanded.

She grinned ruefully. "No. He's not close to my taste." Knowing they wanted an explanation, Eliza breathed deeply and plunged into the story. "My adoptive parents died in a horrific accident caused by a drunk driver going the wrong way – fast – on the freeway and hitting their car head on. The human news broadcast the story immediately. After completing the investigation, the story surfaced again with more details. The perpetrator survived with relatively minor injuries and ended up criminally charged and convicted, causing the press to continue covering the story. His very wealthy family had turned a blind eye to his alcoholism—"

Mrs. Claus exclaimed, "That's why you asked Lugh about leprechauns' problem with alcohol!"

Eliza nodded, tearing up. "Yes. That's a very touchy subject with me." She paused, glancing around the table and ending at her dad. "Lawyers recognized an opportunity at a civil lawsuit that was an open and shut case. They pestered me relentlessly, encouraging me to sue the wealthy family. My adoptive parents had planned well for me, and I had plenty of money because of their advance efforts. I didn't need more, and I didn't believe in making the wealthy family pay. Nothing could give me what I wanted – my adoptive parents back."

"What happened?" Santa prompted.

"A very smart lawyer suggested I approach the situation with a different attitude. 'This is a chance for you to help those who need it,' he stated. 'Put whatever you get from the lawsuit into a foundation that doles out assistance to whatever causes you feel appropriate. You can be a force for good. In an odd way you can honor your parents and channel money from the wealthy family to good.'"

"While I don't believe money solves all problems, many do need it badly. I mulled over his point. I did not like the personal attention I received due to the prominence of the story in the human news. I wanted out of the spotlight." She smiled at her dad. "I decided to take his advice. After a quick trial, the jury awarded a much, much greater amount than anticipated. The lawyer walked away set for life, and I established a very well-funded foundation."

She took another deep breath. "Roger's appearance precipitated my building this house and moving here. I wanted to disappear."

"Did he hurt you?" Navva cautiously asked.

Eliza smiled broadly. "Not in the way you are thinking. Out of the blue one day he walked up to me at a coffee shop as I worked on my laptop. 'I've seen you on the news, he stated. You're Eliza. I am, I replied.' Uninvited, he sat down at my table and proceeded to talk incessantly. When I attempted to extricate myself, he asked me out. I turned him down. That began a series of him appearing where I went, following me to clients' offices, and even dropping in at my home. He was stalking me and became more and more obsessed that he was marrying me so that he could get the money from the lawsuit. He created a fake marriage license that he presented to me 'Until we could get the real thing, he said.' Yes, I did tear it up."

"Good for you, Kiddo," Bobby's disembodied voice praised. "I didn't realize you needed out of a situation badly. I am more satisfied than ever I urged you to check out these woods."

"Thank you, Uncle Bobby. I'm sending you a big hug for your efforts."

"So you disappeared?" Navva questioned.

"Yes. Thankfully Roger did not find me for several years."

"While I appreciate Officer Griffin's assistance today, he will not be the answer to the problem Roger presents," Santa declared.

"Good idea to contact him, Dad," Eliza complimented. "Did you ask Blogger to do that?"

Santa nodded. "I did."

Eliza grinned slyly. "He didn't believe my friend was in the house."

"I don't think he did, either," Mrs. Claus agreed.

"How do you plan to handle Roger?" Eliza wondered.

"I'll erase his memory of you," Santa responded. "I'm concerned that when he returns he could hurt you. Be very alert. I'm adding a trigger specific to his presence which will signal me he is near you." He hesitated and then turned to Navva and Teeny Tiny Elf. "Neither one of you may stay here to help Eliza. I don't want you involved in this altercation. You could get injured or inadvertently cause Eliza to be."

Neither one appeared satisfied with Santa's directive. "But, I could—" Teeny Tiny Elf insisted.

Santa cut him off. "No," he stated firmly in a tone which signaled no discussion. Looking at Eliza, he cautioned, "Remember to run your circular-pattern-energy-detector so that Roger doesn't sneak up on you."

Recognizing the gravity of the situation, Eliza readily agreed. "I will, Dad."

Roger's visit left apprehension in his wake and cast a pall over their conversation. Each carried the dish he or she had brought to the deck back to the kitchen. All four kissed Eliza good-bye and advised her to be careful. They left very concerned for her safety.

Chapter 16

When they gathered for the third interview, Mittka continued on his good behavior, materializing about the same time as the four from the North Pole. Giving Eliza another abbreviated kiss, he moved to Mrs. Claus and Teeny Tiny Elf, attempting to honor Santa's request and spreading his attention around in order to diffuse Navva's tension. Patrick and Robin were quite excited when they appeared.

"We were able to get an interview with a wise acacias tree deva in the savannah of Africa," Patrick announced. "Let's go immediately. Santa, would you please—"

"Right away."

They arrived to the moisture-laden air of summer.

Eliza looked up at the tree underneath which they stood. Its bare, leafless trunk rose quite a distance to an umbrella top. "This species of tree is often included in scenes of Africa taken by humans," she noted.

"You're right," agreed Robin. "We were excited to get an interview because this wise tree deva will tell you a great deal about trees' senses."

"Senses?" Eliza repeated. "Do you mean smell, taste, hearing, touch, and sight?"

"Yes," Robin replied. "Which senses do you think trees use?"

Encouraged by praise during the second interview, Navva jumped in. "None of those."

Eliza smiled at Navva. "I agree with Navva."

"We are about to change your view of trees dramatically, then," Robin informed them.

Patrick addressed the tree. "Thank you for granting us an interview today." Pointing to each as he introduced, Patrick continued, "We are pleased to have Mittka along, plus Santa, Mrs. Claus, their daughter Eliza who is writing the book, their family members Teeny Tiny Elf, and Navva."

"What an illustrious group! I am honored to welcome you to my home," remarked the acacias tree full of yellow blooms.

Getting right to the point as usual, Eliza asked, "What sense do you use frequently?"

"Smell."

"Really? How do you use it?"

"Occasionally giraffes decide to nibble on my leaves. When a herd appears, I send out a warning ethylene gas which tells the other acacias trees in the vicinity of the giraffes' presence."

"What happens then?" Eliza wondered.

"They detect the gas and in response we all release a toxic substance into our leaves which discourages the giraffes from munching on them. The wind helps us by carrying our gaseous scent message around the area."

"And you save your leaves from being destroyed," Eliza added.

"That's right."

Staring at the tree's bright yellow flowers, Eliza was reminded of fairies. "Do trees use scent to attract pollinators?"

"Of course," the acacias tree agreed. "You are familiar with the blossoms of fruit trees dispersing scents into the air for that purpose, but many other trees have blossoms with lesser known scents which do the same."

"Okay, so I get the scent," Eliza noted. "What other senses do you use?"

"We use taste to discourage or kill predators."

"Such as the giraffes?"

"Yes, but in other ways. We can identify the presence of an insect from its saliva, which we taste."

Eliza was intrigued. "You taste the insect's saliva?! What do you do then?"

"We have several ways to respond depending upon the insect. We can summon predators who find the insects delicious to help by devouring them. We send those signals by smell. Sometimes the predators are other insects which we alert via electrical impulses."

"You use electrical impulses?!" Navva exclaimed.

"Our electricity only travels at a third of an inch per minute, but that works for trees," the acacias tree maintained. "As you know, we move at a slow pace."

"Wow!" Eliza declared. "Are your electrical impulses carried in the air, too?"

"Sometimes," the tree replied. "Some are sent through our root or fungi networks." It paused. "According to Robin, in the last interview you learned about cooperation between trees. The fungi networks give us opportunities to communicate with the roots of single trees which may be touched by the fungi network but not by other trees' roots."

"So the fungi are helpful?" Eliza questioned. "I thought those could be destructive to trees."

"Usually they are helpful. If a tree is weakened, the fungi could allow destructive microbes in. Whether the fungi are positive or negative for the individual tree depends upon the tree's condition, which is not brought on by the fungi."

"So the fungi don't necessarily initiate a problem, but they could add to one?" Eliza clarified.

"Yes. You will likely be surprised to know that we produce chemicals on demand which are deadly or disruptive to the insects attacking us."

"You create chemicals compounds at will?" Eliza turned to Patrick. "You and Robin are correct; my world view regarding trees is rapidly changing."

"One last sense – for now," the tree noted. "I don't want to give you too much at once. Robin shared that you sing to your trees. Trees react to sound."

"That one doesn't surprise me. I feel my trees' contentment when I am singing," Eliza revealed.

"We eavesdropped on human scientists who recently recorded seedlings' roots leaning toward sound produced at 220 hertz." The tree halted. "Much to their astonishment, they discovered our reaction to sound."

Eliza smiled. "Perhaps I ought to have a talk with the scientists."

"That's a very good idea," the acacias tree deva praised.

"If I thought they would listen," she assessed, "I would. Any more?"

"That's just a small sample of trees' senses of smell, taste, visual, touch, and sound. More will be revealed soon. In the meantime, your readers can find out more about trees by communicating with them as you do."

"Excellent point! They can discover how to talk to trees and hear them by meditating. I'll include that in the book," she vowed.

"Thank you," the acacias deva finished.

"Thank you!" Eliza returned. "What a riveting interview. I learned a lot."

After everyone had spoken with the tree, thanked it, and bid good-bye, Santa transported them back to Eliza's. Patrick and Robin's excitement has zoomed. "What an informative interview!" Patrick exuded.

"We wanted to cover that material for the book but couldn't find the right tree deva to give it. Please note to your readers that the acacias tree deva resides in Africa but spoke about trees in its home and other areas," Robin noted.

"I will," Eliza assured him.

"I'm off!" Mittka offered as he disappeared.

"I have a meeting with the Growing Grounds staff on the Nona concoction," Mrs. Claus explained. Giving her daughter a kiss, she smiled. "We'll see you in a couple of days."

Santa and Teeny Tiny Elf each kissed Eliza, too, and offered good-byes.

Navva was last. Giving Eliza a loving kiss, he whispered, "Good job. I understand why your books are so good. You pull out information with probing questions."

"Thank you," she murmured, initiating a loving kiss back.

As the North Pole group transported, Patrick and Robin also waved good-bye and disappeared.

That afternoon, Eliza had work for her clients that she interspersed with housework. Shifting her focus between the two she became totally absorbed and didn't notice her visitor until he whirled her around, took the laundry basket out of her hands, set it down, and pulled her close. Covering her lips with his, he engaged her in a long loving kiss.

When he finally moved his lips slightly off hers, he

breathed deeply. "An abbreviated kiss in the morning is not enough," Mittka admitted. "I am desperately trying to follow your dad's request, but each day I am finding more difficulty doing so."

"Is that why you leave as soon as we return?"

"You noticed." His gaze fell on her lips and once again his mouth hungrily latched onto hers in another long kiss.

Acting like someone who had walked across the desert and couldn't get enough water, he moved his lips off hers just enough to talk. "You are intoxicating," he mumbled.

Cupping his face in her hands, she empathized, "I am complimented. While I don't intend to brush you off, I am in the middle of several tasks. Let's share one more kiss and you leave so I can finish what I am doing."

He implored, "Would you take time for more?"

She shook her head. "No," she stated firmly, covering his lips with hers for one final kiss.

He clung to her extra long and for a couple seconds she wondered if he would ever pull away. Finally, he did, smiled, and disappeared, leaving Eliza with an unsettled feeling.

Chapter 17

The morning of the fourth interview, Patrick and Robin showed up first, partly to interrupt Mittka. The North Pole group arrived a few seconds later. When Mittka appeared, Patrick and Robin flanked him, requesting of Santa, "We're ready. Would you—"

Picking up their intent, Santa transported them without saying a word. They materialized in a grove of deciduous trees. Robin turned to Eliza. "How do trees propagate?"

Caught off guard, Eliza hesitated. After thinking for a bit, she answered, "I don't know much about that. The oaks with me drop acorns which sprout into seedlings—"

"How often do they produce acorns?" Patrick questioned.

"Every year."

"Do you notice the same number every year?"

Eliza halted. "I don't know. I've never counted. They give the impression of being the same to me."

Robin seemed pleased. "We thought how trees propagate was likely a little understood part of tree life. Your answers indicate we were correct."

"We'll start with trees' methods of birth control," Patrick continued.

"They do seem to produce a lot of acorns," Eliza agreed, "probably too many – but birth control? Really?"

"Look around. All the trees in this woods bloom at the same time," Robin stated. "They agreed to do that."

"Why?" Navva wondered.

"In order to reproduce, trees use nourishment they need for survival. They exercise caution to apply their reproductive efforts wisely so that they achieve success without endangering their own health. Toward that end, they synchronize their reproductive frequency, which is different every year," Patrick explained.

"So the trees in my woods do not drop the same number of acorns each year?" Eliza asked.

"No."

"Why vary the number?" Navva inserted. "Wouldn't they have less stress if they produced a smaller number consistently?"

"That's a good point," Mittka replied. "However their stress is not the main issue; predators are."

Perplexed, Eliza repeated, "Predators of trees?"

Mittka flashed a beguiling smile. "Predators of acorns," he corrected, "which in your woods, and here, are deer. They love indulging in acorns to fatten up for winter."

"If trees released the same number of acorns each year, the deer would adapt and consume all of them. By changing the frequency, the deer get confused, don't find many one season, and give up on seeking out the little nuts. The deer realize they cannot consistently count on acorns for nourishment," Robin expounded.

"The following season when the deer have curtailed their search, the trees drop a bunch," Mittka added, "offering that seasons' crop a better chance to avoid the predators' delighting in them."

"Do the trees get together every year and agree when and how much they will bloom? That's their birth control?" Eliza clarified.

"You're right," Mittka affirmed. "As a community, the trees around us decide each year whether to reproduce or not. They want to keep their reproductive efforts irregular to throw the deer off balance."

Eliza shrieked, "Whether to reproduce or not? Are you telling us that some years they do not reproduce? They can adjust their reproduction so much that they turn it off completely?"

Smiling at her astonishment, Mittka nodded. "Yes, that is exactly what I am saying."

She stared at him in shock. She had never heard of the ability to turn reproduction off at will. Finally, she found a question. "Has irregularity caused problems for the trees?"

"And for bees," Mittka noted. "Trees' inconsistency deprives bees of the benefits of pollination from trees. That prompted bees to seek other pollination resources and trees to seek other ways to be pollinated." He looked at Navva. "Any ideas what replaced the bee as trees' main pollinator?"

Navva stared at Mittka, thinking. Suddenly he burst out, "Wind! The wind proved a more consistent resource, didn't have a danger of dying off, and could swirl pollen from tree to tree, within a group of trees, or even throughout a woods."

"Right on!" Mittka praised, offering Navva a high-five. Navva was so pleased with himself that he returned the high-five without realizing he shared it with Mittka. "The wind does offer a bonus not found with bees in that it carries the pollen further, thereby giving the trees more genetic diversity."

Eliza glanced down and noticed a young six-inch high oak at her feet. She bent down, stroking the little oak lovingly. "Once an acorn becomes this, does it get any help from the trees around it?"

"When a seed falls from a tree, every species has a strategy as to how the seed sprouts," Patrick responded. "If the seed settles onto soft, damp soil such as that one did, it may sprout immediately."

Robin continued, "Some seeds wait a season or more to sprout. Although that leaves them at the risk of being a tasty morsel for a hungry deer, it gives them the option of holding back during a dry spring."

"Their option of delay also spreads the risk of a seed's not making it over a couple of years so that all seeds are not lost in one season," Mittka noted. "Some trees give their seeds up to five years to germinate."

Eliza's shock perpetuated. "So the seed can determine germination, too?"

Mittka looked intently at Eliza. She could tell his not receiving a kiss this morning had worn thin. Taking a deep breath, he added, "Um hum. In addition, the parents do all they can to regulate the young one's growth by adjusting how much sunlight it receives."

"Are they concerned about it growing too fast?" Eliza wondered.

"Yes," Patrick confirmed. "Slow growth when a tree is young helps it live a healthy life and reach old age. A young tree's woody cells are very small and do not have air inside, giving them flexibility to bend as needed during storms."

The trees nearby, which had been silent during their conversation, spoke. "We are very concerned about our young ones," offered a mature tree.

"Every year of our existence we watch those that are growing and do what we can to hold them back so that they develop at a slow pace," contributed another.

"Just like in my woods, I see many small ones around our feet. How many of them will survive?" Eliza queried.

"We know from our experience and that of our parents," a third tree answered, "that each one of us will be survived by one of our children."

"Really?" Eliza cried. "You put out all those acorns and only one will grow to maturity like you? I'm sad for you."

"We're not sad about one reaching our age," explained

a fourth. "We are thrilled one does. As you understand, the odds are against us, particularly with humans logging and building homes in the woods."

"Consider the available space," offered a fifth. "We don't have room for us to be replaced by several children. If we were, our offspring would be crowded and unhealthy, likely dying off before their offspring had a chance to mature."

"We want our woods to survive," stated a sixth.

"And thrive," concluded a seventh.

Eliza was astounded by trees' propagation methods, regulation of seeds and young trees, and attitudes toward survival. "Thank you, Patrick, Robin, Mittka, and the trees around us for giving me this information. I think readers will find your actions and perspectives fascinating."

Teeny Tiny Elf hopped from tree to tree of those that had concluded the interview, giving each a hug. "Yes, thank you, wonderful trees. We appreciate you!"

Returning to Eliza, he jumped into her arms. "I had no idea about everything that was discussed today!"

Santa, Mrs. Claus, and Navva echoed Teeny Tiny Elf's comment and added their appreciation. They arrived back at Eliza's kitchen speechless. Mittka immediately said "Good-bye" and disappeared, barely restraining himself from grabbing Eliza in a kiss before he left.

Robin revealed, "We have excitedly been maintaining a very non-tree pace of every two days. In deference to trees, and you, we are dropping back to every three days with four interviews left. Does that work for all of you?"

Eliza opened her schedule, noting three, then six, then, nine, and finally twelve days from that date. "I'm good." Glancing at her parents and Navva, she asked, "Do you three have plans that would interfere with specific dates?"

Her mother smiled. "Our schedules tend to be more flexible than yours, Dear."

Santa chuckled. "We want to go to Nona soon to check on the children but will fit that in between these excursions."

"I hope I have time to go," Eliza exclaimed. "I would love to see them!"

After everyone left, Eliza had a quick lunch and dove into writing that day's contribution to the book. Since he had been denied a kiss this morning, she fully expected to see Mittka. When he didn't show, she was relieved. Maybe he's getting a grip on himself, she mused.

Chapter 18

Suddenly, Eliza remembered that she was out of dog food and needed some for that evening. She rushed to her car. "My keys!" she exclaimed as she reached for the car door. "I forgot my keys!"

She also forgot to run her circular-energy-pattern detector. She turned, intending to retrieve her keys from the house. Roger slammed her hard and fast. Eliza crumpled against her car, leaving a trail of blood as she slid to the garage floor. On her way, she grasped to steady herself, touching Roger's face and raking her nails over his left cheek.

His blood from her scratches dripping on Eliza, he grabbed her by the collar and slapped her unconscious face six times, pouring out his anger. "That's for giving me a lot of trouble!"

He received so much satisfaction from his action that he added three more. "And that's for disappearing and making me track you down!"

After binding her hands and feet to prevent her from moving, he tossed her unconscious form into the back of his truck. He smiled in anticipation. "We'll have a little fun back here when you wake up."

He ran his hand over the gun he had set on the truck bed for easy access. "If you don't want to cooperate, we'll be where no one will hear what happens next. If you do go along, we'll get married, and I'll finally have my money and you to boot!"

Hurriedly jumping into the driver's seat, Roger started his truck and sped down the driveway. He turned onto the main road just as Santa materialized in Eliza's garage. Santa immediately spied the blood on Eliza's car. Touching it, he replayed what had just happened. Watching Roger slap Eliza's senseless face caused Santa's solar plexus to tighten. He felt sick.

Knowing he had to wait until Roger stopped to trace their location, Santa telepathically contacted Mrs. Claus. *Roger has Eliza. She's unconscious. He left with her in his truck.*

As soon as they stop, I will find them. I'll bring her back to her bedroom.

She immediately materialized beside Santa. Noticing the blood on Eliza's car, she also touched it and replayed the attack. She turned pale. "Our poor baby!" she cried. Leaning her head on Santa's shoulder, she sobbed.

He held her comfortingly. "I'm thankful I added the trigger of his presence to her," Santa mumbled. "I was worried about just this type of incident."

Bobby's disembodied voice added, "I'm glad you did, too, Bro. Roger is one nasty individual who has very bad intentions. Careful, he has a gun, too."

"I'm not surprised," Santa remarked.

Roger had staked out a remote park. After visiting it several times, he had confirmed the park had little use, particularly during the week. Being Tuesday, he had every confidence he would not be disturbed with what he wanted to do to Eliza. Pulling in, he chose the most hidden parking spot tucked under an overhang of trees.

Roger stopped his truck, pulled out his keys, and shoved open the door, consumed with excitement as he rushed to the back of his truck. Dropping the tailgate, he chuckled gleefully at the sight of Eliza's inert body. Pressing his right hand on the tailgate to hoist his body onto the truck bed, Roger felt the strongest grip across his chest he had ever encountered. "What—"

Before he could finish his sentence, Santa ran his hand across Roger's forehead, erasing his memory of Eliza and causing Roger to black out. Santa allowed Roger's body to slump onto the pavement, finishing by carefully resting Roger's head on the hard surface. Settling onto the tailgate, Santa eased Eliza toward him. Noting the slap marks on her face and the dried blood, tears filled Santa's eyes. "I'm sorry you received this treatment, our precious daughter. I'm sorry."

Untying the bindings on Eliza's hands and feet, Santa gently slid his arms underneath her, cradling her against his chest. They transported into Eliza's bedroom where Mrs. Claus waited anxiously.

Santa stretched Eliza out on her bed. "Let me wipe off her face, Dear, before you heal those marks," Mrs. Claus suggested.

To Santa's nod, Mrs. Claus lovingly stroked Eliza's face with the cloth, removing any trace of blood or grime.

When she was done, Santa placed his hands on Eliza's face, healing her tissue and eliminating signs of Roger's handslaps. Then Santa checked her for a concussion. "If she has a concussion, it is a light one," Santa concluded.

"How long until she wakes up, Dear?" Mrs. Claus wondered.

"Hard to tell."

"Why don't you stay with her? I'll start dinner. Let me know if she stirs, and I will be right here."

"Good idea. She'll likely be hungry when she comes to."

Eliza awakened in a disoriented state. Her eyes still closed, she stretched. Her hand dropped onto Santa's knee. She opened her eyes and exclaimed, "Dad, what are you doing here?"

"What do you remember?"

She stared at him blankly for a couple seconds. "I rushed to get to the store…"

Mrs. Claus had been on the alert for voices. Hearing them, she immediately went to Eliza's bedroom. Eliza spotted her. "Hi, Mom! Why are you here?" Eliza paused. "Okay, something must have happened. I remember that I had forgotten my car keys and turned to go back into the house." She halted again. Looking back at her dad, she stated, "I don't remember anything after that."

"That's probably a good thing," Santa began and proceeded to tell what they had watched on the replay and his rescue. As he finished, Eliza sat up, embraced him, and planted a big kiss on his cheek. "Wonderful Father, thank you for looking out for me. Absorbed in my rush I didn't run my circular-energy-pattern-detector. Sorry."

"While activating that is important, you are not responsible for Roger's behavior. He is. I'm thankful he interrupted our lunch a few days ago so that I knew of his existence." He hesitated. "Do you have any more like him lurking in your background? Any old boyfriends? Anybody who you denied seeing? I had not thought to ask you those questions, but now they are pressing on my psyche."

Mrs. Claus had settled down on the bed across from her husband. "Your father won't phrase his question this way, but we both recognize your beauty, Dear, and know you could attract men without trying."

Glancing from her mother to her dad, Eliza smiled. "I love you both so much for so many reasons. You just exhibited one of them. I cannot think of anyone who could be direct with a question and yet craft it in a gentle, caring fashion." She looked at her dad. "To answer your question, Dad, not that I know of. Although my beauty Mother references could have drawn some of which I am unaware."

"Let's hope we get advance warning if they exist,"

Santa replied. "How do you feel? Do you have a headache or any other pains?"

She started to shake her head and grimaced. Santa noticed. "I'll fix that." He stood and adjusted her neck and shoulders. "Try moving now. Is that better?"

"Yes. Thank you."

"Would you like dinner, Dear?" Mrs. Claus offered.

"Absolutely." Extending her hand, she asked Santa, "Would you help me up, Dad? I feel slightly off. I'd appreciate your help to the kitchen."

Santa flashed a broad smile. "I love the opportunity to give you support."

Taking their seats at the table, Mrs. Claus stated, "We are staying the night, Dear, to be certain you don't have any lasting effects. Thankfully, Navva spent the afternoon with Justine and Ilya. He planned to have dinner with them and his parents. In order not to disturb us, he informed us as he left that he would stay with them tonight. "

Eliza sighed. "So you don't have to share this incident with him. I'm glad. He's riled up enough about Mittka. He doesn't need to think about Roger, too." Glancing from Santa to Mrs. Claus, she added, "Thank you both."

Roger revived in the darkness. Where am I? He thought.

He felt a cold breeze blowing across his bare chest. His hands touched pavement. Stretching up, his knuckles hit the hard tailgate. "Ouch!" he cried.

Rising to his feet, he stumbled along the side of his truck until he found the driver's door. Opening it, he squinted at the bright light. He fumbled in his pocket and discovered his keys. He felt a little woozy but started the truck anyway and roared out of the parking lot. Uncertain of his location, he meandered around until he saw a gas station. Just in time, he thought. I was almost out of gas.

After filling his tank, he walked to the building. Inside a police officer stood by the counter, talking to the clerk. Roger interrupted, "How do I find the freeway?"

"I thought I told you to leave this area," Officer Griffin stated.

Roger exclaimed, "Who are you? I've never met you."

"You were trespassing on Eliza's property." He noticed the scratch marks on Roger's face. "Where did you get those scratches on your face?"

Putting his hand up to his face, Roger felt his dried blood and the pain. "Ouch!" he cried. "I don't know. Where is your restroom?"

Unsteadily walking in the direction the clerk pointed, Roger entered the room and instantly looked in the mirror. "Wow!" He exclaimed aloud. "Where did I get those? Did an animal attack me?"

Scared, he exited the room and shakily returned to the counter. "I don't know," he answered Officer Griffin. "I want outta here. Don't worry, I'm leaving and not coming back."

Officer Griffin's brow furrowed. His suspicions had been aroused. Did Eliza give him those scratches? Had she been hurt? Why did he act disoriented?

He decided to drive over to Eliza's. He arrived to an open garage door. His lights shone on dried blood. What had happened? He wondered.

Officer Griffin rang the doorbell.

Santa answered the door. "Good evening, Officer Griffin. What brings you here tonight?"

"I was at the gas station and encountered that guy Roger who was bothering Eliza. He had scratches on his face. I noticed dried blood on Eliza's car when I drove up just now. Is she okay?"

Santa smiled. "Thank you for your concern. Yes, she is okay. Would you like to talk to her?"

"I would."

"Follow me." Santa led Officer Griffin into the kitchen where Mrs. Claus and Eliza sat at the table, the plates in front of them filled with dinner. "Officer Griffin is here to check on you, Eliza. He met Roger at a gas station and noticed scratches on his face."

Eliza smiled. "Thank you for your concern, Officer Griffin. I appreciate you." She paused. "Roger probably got into another altercation."

"I noticed your open garage and saw dried blood on your car, which worried me greatly."

Thinking quickly, Eliza apologized, "I'm sorry. I had gone to the store and exited the car juggling too many packages. The blood from some fresh meat dribbled onto my car. Mother and Dad surprised me with dinner so I haven't cleaned it up yet."

"Would you like to join us for dinner, Officer Griffin?" Mrs. Claus invited.

"I'm just about done with my shift and will be headed home shortly, but, thanks, anyway."

Rising, Mrs. Claus changed her offer. "Take some with you. Your wife would appreciate your bringing some home. We have plenty."

"Dinner smells delicious," he acknowledged. "You are right. I'm sure she would appreciate not having to cook."

Mrs. Claus had already begun assembling his to-go package. "Just the two of you?"

"We have a little boy who is three. He doesn't eat much."

"I've included extra," Mrs. Claus noted. "I hope you enjoy it."

Convinced that more had gone on than these three were admitting, Officer Griffin accepted the food and left. His wife was thrilled he brought home dinner. Neither one had ever had a meal that tasty.

Chapter 19

Santa, Mrs. Claus, and Eliza kept Roger's attack to themselves with one exception. On their way home the day after, Santa and Mrs. Claus stopped by Grandfather and Nanna's.

Santa had telepathically contacted them before leaving Eliza's. *We have news. May we stop by shortly?*

Sure. See you soon, Grandfather had replied.

Grandfather and Nanna were waiting expectantly when Santa and Mrs. Claus materialized just outside their door. Thrilled to see Mrs. Claus, Nanna exclaimed, "You both came! What a pleasure."

After welcoming hugs and kisses, all four settled at the kitchen table where Nanna had tea and fresh cookies waiting. Santa chuckled. "My favorite, again?"

Nanna joined his laughter. "I seem to know when you will be coming. I haven't made these since your last visit."

"I have been so busy lately helping the residents of Nona that I haven't made cookies for a while. Santa doesn't complain, but I'm sure he appreciates yours more than usual," Mrs. Claus commented.

Covering his wife's hand with his own, Santa smiled. "You're right on all counts."

Very curious, Grandfather prompted, "What is your news?"

With a few insertions from Mrs. Claus, Santa related the entire episode with Roger, concluding with his beating and kidnapping Eliza the day before. "Poor Eliza!" Nanna cried when he finished.

Grandfather looked intently at Santa. "Did Mittka show up?"

Santa knew exactly why Grandfather asked. "Yes. He, too, appears to be reacting to Eliza's red energy. Beginning with a kiss at the Project Committee meeting, he visited her alone the afternoon after the meeting and managed to get three more. Patrick and Robin invited him on their excursions about tree devas. Based on their invitation, he has been accompanying us on every excursion and kissing Eliza as soon as he transports in."

"He kisses only Eliza?" Grandfather probed.

"No, he kisses me and Teeny Tiny Elf, too," Mrs. Claus answered.

"Teeny Tiny Elf?!" Nanna repeated.

"He likes Mittka's kisses but on the cheek," Mrs. Claus clarified.

Santa smiled. "To lighten Navva's mood, Teeny Tiny Elf has been encouraging Navva to receive a kiss from Mittka."

Grandfather chuckled. "Leave it to Teeny Tiny Elf. Has that worked?"

"A couple days ago, Mittka did praise Navva for a comment he made and ended with a kiss on Navva's cheek," Mrs. Claus noted, "but Navva wiped it off."

"Eliza has this coming at her from every direction," Grandfather identified. "You said Mittka visited her privately after the Project Committee meeting. Has that happened since?"

Santa shook his head. "Not that I know."

"Have you asked Eliza?"

"No. I hadn't considered that. I've been focused on Navva."

"Does Navva know what happened yesterday?" Nanna wondered.

"No," Mrs. Claus replied. "Thankfully, he had visited his sister, her fiancé, and his parents yesterday afternoon and evening."

Grandfather addressed Santa. "Do you plan to tell him?"

"I don't think that is wise right now. Do you agree?"

Thinking the situation over, Grandfather took a while to respond. "I do. Navva knowing will likely stir his red energy even more. He will see what we see but through a blood red filter. That would pile one more instance on top of the daily Mittka kisses, which may be too much."

"You are right to be focused on Navva," added Nanna. "I feel he is about to explode."

"Yes, I am very concerned that unwittingly Mittka is pushing Navva over the edge," Santa agreed.

"Is that Mittka's aim?" Grandfather wondered.

"At the beginning I think Mittka just did what he does, kiss anyone who will accept it," Santa commented. "When he realized Navva's reaction, he gained an additional reason to kiss Eliza, and that was to tease Navva."

Mrs. Claus picked up the story. "We both recognize that Mittka has become a victim of his own game. He is addicted to Eliza's kisses and increasingly obsessed with having more and more."

Nanna gasped. "That is dangerous for both."

"Yes," Santa concurred. "Since Roger's episode in the last twenty-four hours, I am speculating Mittka has fallen into red energy that has been exacerbated by Eliza's power. Mittka is always surrounded by red energy, but he has never experienced the heightened level of red energy around Eliza. Even though he and I discussed the red energy which likely attached to her from Pan, he doesn't know of Eliza's power. I suspect that unknown to her she's expanding the red energy's effect."

"We're all discovering her power's impact," Mrs. Claus added.

"That's right, Dear," Santa agreed.

"Thank you," Grandfather acknowledged, "for keeping us informed. I find your suspicions about Eliza's power exacerbating the red energy's effect interesting. The situation has ballooned since our first conversation. We don't have more clarity on Navva, but we are realizing the pressure he is receiving from the red energy around Eliza."

"I hope his explosion is not directed at Eliza," Nanna remarked. "She's already had too much."

Santa looked at Grandfather. "I'll follow up on Mittka's afternoon visits."

"Good idea."

They parted company more unsettled than ever about Eliza's safety, Navva's emotional health, and Mittka's obsession.

Eliza used the three days to recover from Roger's attack. By the following day, Santa's healing touch had dissipated most of Eliza's bruising. Two days later she didn't show any sign of it and felt fully recovered. Once again Patrick and Robin arrived first and immediately flanked Mittka upon his materializing, not giving him a chance to kiss anyone. The group from the North Pole was last. Robin instantly directed Santa, "I have the coordinates in mind."

Materializing at their destination, Mittka asked in a frustrated tone, "What is today's topic?'"

"Trees, carbon dioxide, and their combined effect upon the planet," Patrick replied.

Glancing around, Eliza gasped. "Carbon dioxide didn't do this!"

They stood in the remnants of a forest that had been leveled by a wildfire. "No, it didn't," Patrick agreed, "but the fire released it." He paused. "Follow me."

He led them to a small group of trees at the edge of the burn. They appeared to have been able to survive. Eliza walked up to three. Briefly running her hand down a segment of bark on each, she inquired, "Will you make it?"

The first she had touched offered, "Thank you for your concern. The fire happened last year so we have survived one season. We are feeling quite good and hope to continue."

"You can understand us?" shrieked the second one. "Wow! Yes, thank you for your concern. Are you here to ask about carbon dioxide?"

"Yes, we are," answered Robin. "We appreciate your willingness to talk to us about it."

"We had quite a dose of carbon dioxide during and after the fire," volunteered the third.

"I've heard about carbon dioxide's negative effect on the planet and something about how trees can help, but I've never understood the combination of carbon dioxide, trees, and climate. Would you please explain their effect?" Eliza requested.

"You read my mind," Patrick stated. "I was about to do that." He halted. "You understand photosynthesis, correct?"

Eliza nodded. "I do."

"For your readers' sake, I will give you an explanation to use," Patrick continued. "Trees and plants use light energy, generally from sunlight, to convert water, minerals, and carbon dioxide into what humans would term food."

"Nourishment for their survival," Mrs. Claus clarified.

"Exactly," Patrick praised. "Technically, the form is hydrocarbons. Whatever trees don't use at the time of production is stored in their trunks, branches, and root system. Over a lifetime they store up to twenty-two tons of this nourishment as carbon dioxide, making the forest a huge carbon dioxide cleaner that continually filters out and stores carbon dioxide from the air."

"Wow!" Eliza exclaimed. "That's a lot!" She gestured toward the burned area. "What happened to the carbon dioxide stored in the trees which burned down?"

Robin responded. "The carbon dioxide in the live trees went into the atmosphere and much of what had been stored has been let go since the fire."

Patrick finished, "When a tree dies of old age, its stores are broken down by fungi and bacteria. While some carbon dioxide from those trees goes back into the air, most of it stays in the forest floor. Rain pushes it deeper into the soil, slowly washing it down to cooler regions where its decomposition decelerates."

"In a situation like ours," the first tree near Eliza mentioned, "that process is reversed."

"How?"

"Most forest floors are perpetually shaded by the trees in residence," the second noted. "When the trees' shade is gone, sunlight reaches the soil directly, stimulating the microorganisms there to process decomposing leaves and other plant materials faster, which releases stored gases, particularly carbon dioxide."

"We feel the results because the stores which had been built up are no longer available to us. They're gone. Our stores are being depleted as fast as they form," the third one noted.

"Oh, that's awful!" Eliza cried.

"From what I recall, coal, oil, and gas came over millions of years from the stores you are referencing," Navva remarked. "With stores being dispelled, those that had been untouched, resulting in the formation of coal, oil, and gas, are not around, right?"

"You are correct," the first tree agreed. "Those fuels came from trees which lived near swamps millions of years ago and fell into the water when they died. The water and shade of living trees protected the dead trees' decomposition from sunlight. The substances turned loose from their breakdown remained in the soil, sank deeper and deeper, and were pressurized into what is termed fossil fuels."

"So how does the release of more carbon dioxide into the atmosphere affect trees? Wouldn't you receive more for growth?" Eliza questioned. "Do we need to replenish coal and fossil fuel stores?"

Patrick noted, "Trees today are growing faster than we have ever recorded due to the extra carbon dioxide available."

"You have probably heard this on other interviews. We trees love slow growth. We benefit the environment and humans when we are allowed to grow and live slowly. That applies to our physical remnants after death, too," the third tree contributed. "Slow decomposition protects what is in the soil from being dispelled into the atmosphere."

"So whenever trees are destroyed, the land they protected with their presence and shade is exposed and sets free into the atmosphere what it held?" Eliza summarized.

"Very good!" complimented the second tree. "You got it."

"What difference does that make?" Navva wondered.

"The stores living trees retain in the soil stash away carbon dioxide, keeping it out of the air, offering more oxygen, and reducing the effects of excess carbon dioxide," Robin explained.

Patrick added, "Even though trees grow slowly, human scientists have recently discovered that what humans consider older trees, which to us are trees in mid-life, are full of energy and highly productive, pulling in more carbon dioxide than young trees. Trees with trunks at least three feet in diameter generated three times as much biomass as others that were half as wide."

"Consequently, we would be smart to protect mature and older trees," Eliza concluded.

"Yes," Patrick, Robin, and Mittka responded in unison.

The group had received a great deal of information. As they offered "Thank you" to the three trees, everyone focused on what they had heard. When they materialized in Eliza's kitchen, they remained caught up in those thoughts. Flashing Eliza a look of longing, Mittka disappeared without a word.

Only Eliza noticed.

In a rare preview, Robin disclosed, "In three days we will address the effect trees have on water flow around the planet."

"I hope by then I have processed what we just learned," Eliza confessed. "I think I now understand trees, carbon dioxide, and climate. Fascinating! Thank you very much, Patrick and Robin."

"See you then," Patrick finalized as he and Robin vanished.

Eliza slid her arm around Navva and gave him a loving kiss. "Thanks for your comments today. Could I reward you, Mother, Dad, and Teeny Tiny Elf with lunch? I have it ready."

Returning her kiss, he smiled. "Sounds good to me."

Once again, she sent everyone out to the deck carrying a dish. She tagged along behind with the plates, napkins, and tableware. They had an enjoyable lunch without interruption. Inwardly sighing with relief, Santa and Mrs. Claus were grateful for a calm day.

After they left, Eliza headed to her office to write that day's contribution to the book on tree devas. She had barely begun when she heard her office door swish open. A familiar figure stood in the doorway. He devoured her lips hungrily with his gaze. She smiled. "I've been expecting you."

He moved so quickly to her side that she only had time to stand before he seized her, clamping her arms to her sides as he wrapped her in a passionate embrace. Instantly pressing his lips against Eliza's, Mittka gave her the longest, strongest kiss yet. Lifting his lips slightly off hers in order to take a breath, he mumbled, "Oh, you are satisfying…"

Before she could reply, he covered her mouth with even more intensity. Reflecting his satisfaction, a few minutes later he relaxed his clamp on her arms enough to free them. She pulled away. "Your desire appears to be growing," she commented.

Unable to take his eyes off her face, he agreed. "You are right. The more I have of you, the more I want."

She smiled. "Well, that's all you are getting today. I want to continue what I am doing."

With a pleading look, he begged, "One more, please?"

"Last time your one more was way too long," she noted. "Make this one quick."

He did. "See you in three days," he stated, preparing to transport.

"If you can't control yourself for a brief kiss in front of Navva, don't do it," Eliza warned. "I don't want him upset."

Without comment, Mittka disappeared.

Uneasy, Eliza contacted Santa. *Dad, would you come to my office right away?*

Without replying, Santa materialized in front of her. He immediately noticed her lips looked different than when their group had returned to the North Pole. They appeared bruised. His eyes narrowed. "Did you have a visitor?"

She nodded. "While I wasn't surprised because he hasn't had a kiss the last two excursions, I am getting concerned."

"Why?"

"He grabs and hold me more tightly and urgently. His kisses are longer, harder, and more demanding. In light of Roger's actions, I am worried about another incident."

Santa took the opportunity to follow up on Grandfather's urging. "You had mentioned Mittka stopping by after the Project Committee meeting. Has he come by in the afternoon other times, too?"

Eliza nodded. "Yes, he has."

"Always requesting kisses?"

"He began requesting. He has morphed into taking without asking first. That seems to be a direct result of not receiving one in the morning."

Santa's silence caused Eliza to continue, "At least his not kissing me in the morning calms Navva. I am thankful to Patrick and Robin for their actions."

"But you are paying for his morning denial by placating him in the afternoon."

Eliza shrugged. "If that helps Navva, I'm willing to do it."

"I sense you are not enjoying Mittka's kisses as you did at first," Santa noted.

She smiled. "At first they were enticing. I was never attracted to him the way I am to Navva. Mittka is fun and full of love. I enjoyed playing with him and teasing him a bit. The complications with Navva have wiped all that away. I am very worried about Navva and do not want to add to his disquiet." She paused. "Too much of anything playful, such as Mittka's kisses, ceases to be fun. That's where I am now."

Santa did not feel ready to share his suspicions that her power was likely exacerbating the red energy attached to her. Although Mittka had gotten more demanding, Santa knew Eliza could handle him. After Roger, she was on the alert. Santa thought the best course was to encourage Eliza to rein in Mittka. Hopefully, that would be enough.

"Have you given Mittka parameters?"

"The last two times I have," she acknowledged. "A few minutes ago I referenced that last time his final kiss was way too long, and he needed to make this one brief."

"Did he?"

"Yes, he did."

"Good. Continue to establish boundaries and make sure he adheres to them."

"What if he doesn't?"

"Use a bolt or a freeze, whichever seems applicable."

"I'm too close to send a bolt. I'd use the freeze. Then what?"

"Contact me. I'll be here immediately."

"Thanks, Dad," she murmured, giving him a hug and a kiss. "I appreciate your advice and help."

He smiled. "What are dads for? I want you to be safe."

Later he shared their conversation with Mrs. Claus. "Her experience with Roger has put her on guard."

"I'm glad she contacted me instead of me questioning her about Mittka."

"She's caught between Mittka's fun-loving actions and Navva's angst," Mrs. Claus noted.

Santa sighed. "I hope we can guide her through without her experiencing more pain."

"Me too, Dear. Me, too."

Chapter 20

Confident that he could satisfy his cravings with Eliza that afternoon, three days later Mittka arrived right on time. Robin and Patrick immediately flanked him. Flashing Eliza a knowing smile, Mitta addressed everyone, "Good Morning, all!" He turned to Patrick and Robin. "So we are talking about trees and water today. Where are we headed?"

In answer Eliza recognized the hum of sylphs. As they appeared, Robin noted, "The sylphs are accompanying us. We are making several stops. They offered to come along and fill in any gaps of our explanation."

Eliza smiled brightly. "Welcome, friends! We are happy to see you!"

"We are excited to contribute to another book," the leader gushed.

Her smile morphing to laughter, Eliza complimented, "I won't be surprised if you are in more books than any other group. Good PR!"

Rapidly fluttering their wings in response, the leader agreed. "That's our aim."

"We are ready, Santa!" Patrick urged.

Santa immediately transported the group to Patrick's destination. Although they stood in the middle of a woods, they could hear ocean waves splashing. Patrick began, "Trees require a great deal of moisture for life. The main source of moisture on this planet is the oceans. As you can hear, we are near one. Since most trees grow on higher ground than oceans, the water they receive from the oceans comes from ocean-water evaporation accumulating in clouds and wind moving the clouds over land to drop rain onto the trees."

"How far can the wind push those rain clouds over land?" Eliza wondered.

"Very good question!" Robin praised. "Not far. Wind pushes ocean-water clouds about four hundred miles inland. The trees in that swath of land are the first link in a process that brings rain into the interior of continents."

He paused. "The canopy of leaves on trees in that stretch offers a huge surface area for the rain to strike. A great deal of the precipitation which hits trees' canopy evaporates before reaching the ground, forming new clouds. The wind moves these clouds further inland where rain once again falls, and the process is repeated over and over, reaching the entire continent."

"Why are we in the midst of a forest on the coast?" Navva questioned. "Wouldn't the ones inland which continue moving the water along be more important?"

"The coastal forests must be viable to start the process," Robin explained. "If the trees in a coastal forest have been decimated, those trees' massive numbers of leaves are missing. They are the first link in the chain. Without the first link, the chain does not exist."

"In Brazil coastal forests are disappearing and the inland Amazonian forests are drying out," Patrick added.

"Oh…" Navva murmured, mulling over the implications.

Patrick caught Santa's eye. "Santa, would you transport us to the second spot?"

Without responding, Santa did.

"Now we are in an interior forest. Keep in mind that a trail of forests to the innermost part of a continent is

226

what establishes and perpetuates a continuous water cycle. If any part of that trail disappears, the water cycle will be disrupted," Patrick emphasized.

"Transpiration from trees' leaves also helps, right?" Eliza asked.

"You are right," Patrick replied. "The trees' roots absorb the rainwater that reaches the ground and send it back up the tree to be released as water vapor through the underside of the leaves. The vapor adds to the cloud cover."

"We learned about transpiration in the Amazon for the book on elves," Eliza noted.

"We sure did!" Teeny Tiny Elf proclaimed. Hopping onto Eliza's arm, he reached for a leaf on a the branch touching her shoulder. Carefully lifting the leaf with one hand, he pointed with the other, "This is where transpiration takes place."

Eliza smiled. "Thank you, Mr. Smarty, for that visual."

"Yes, thank you, Teeny Tiny Elf. You are giving readers of Eliza's books a good refresher," Mittka remarked.

Beaming first at Mittka and then Eliza, Teeny Tiny Elf proudly replied, "You are welcome. I like to help."

"Trees, wherever they are located," Robin stressed, "are a critical part of the water cycle on this planet."

"So is the wind," the lead sylph noted.

Mittka agreed. "Without the wind pushing inland the clouds that are formed from the evaporation off trees, the water cycle would not happen, either. The water cycle is a cooperative effort of several parts of nature, most notably water, trees, and wind."

"After the tornado felled most of the trees in my woods," Eliza remarked, "I have viewed wind as having a negative impact on trees. Your description of the cooperation between the wind and the trees to move water inland is changing my perspective."

"As we have discussed previously," the lead aylph responded, "wind energy can become strong and, therefore, destructive. However, most wind is helpful, especially to trees."

"Next to land masses and rock formations, trees offer a substantial impediment to slow down the wind and make it less destructive to land, plants, and animals," Mrs. Claus noted.

The sylphs concurred.

"Trees help move water through the environment in other ways, too," Patrick added, "the most notable of which is their dead leaves. Leaf build up on the forest floor holds moisture for the soil. Some of the moisture seeps down through the leaf layers and feeds underground springs. Some puddles on the leaves and flows into streams above ground. Wherever and however moisture is distributed, trees likely had a part in its dispersion."

"I truly had never viewed trees as doing that," Eliza offered, amazed.

Glancing at Santa, Navva asked, "Do conifers and deciduous trees participate equally in the water cycle?"

Robin grinned. "Thank you, Navva, for leading us into the third stop. Santa—"

When he received the coordinates, Santa smiled broadly. They arrived to an area familiar to Eliza and Santa – one of the elves' healthy Christmas tree plantings. Indicating the trees around them, Robin complimented, "We are standing in the midst of Santa and the elves' efforts to add more trees to the planet. These are conifers. In answer to your question, Navva, deciduous trees contribute the most to the water cycle because they grow where the water cycle is particularly active."

"We are standing in the environment for conifers. Although this environment does not allow them to participate in the water cycle as deciduous trees do, conifers contribute in their own unique way," Mittka noted.

Patrick picked up the explanation. "Conifers release

an unsaturated hydrocarbon termed terpene. Conifers do this to protect themselves against pests and disease. However, terpenes are also conifers' assist to the water cycle. You see, moisture condenses around terpenes and forms clouds that are twice as thick as the clouds over non-forested areas of conifers' environment."

"Not only does that increase the possibility of precipitation," Robin remarked, "but the clouds reflect about five percent of the sunlight away from the ground near the conifers. That creates a cool, moisture-laden habitat, one the conifers love."

"That brings to mind," Santa inserted, "a statement I have heard. Trees create their own habitat."

"So true!" Robin and Patrick exclaimed in unison.

Tucking Teeny Tiny Elf into her elbow, Eliza strolled over to stand amid several of the planted trees. "How are you?" she cooed softly, brushing her free hand over several branches. Her love emanating to them was palpable to all assembled.

"We're good!" echoed from the ones closest to the ones far away. Her query seemed to have stimulated ripples of gratitude that stirred into waves. For a few minutes the group basked in the goodwill swirling around them.

As Teeny Tiny Elf and Mrs. Claus joined her in touching branches, the trees' appreciation swelled. Soaking in the sentiment, Patrick waited until it abated for his final statement. "We hope we have given your readers an understanding of the significance trees make in distributing water. Any questions?"

Caught up in the trees gratitude, even Navva couldn't come up with one. They transported home overflowing with thanks. Throwing out, "See you next time!" Mittka vanished.

"That was a very informative excursion," Mrs. Claus commented.

"Yes, you planned an excellent presentation," Eliza remarked, "and greatly helped me write this part of the book. Thank you."

"You are welcome," Patrick and Robin acknowledged before disappearing.

Handing Teeny Tiny Elf to Mrs. Claus, Eliza gave her mother a hug and a kiss. After doing the same with Santa, she finished with a loving kiss to Navva. Pulling back slightly, she murmured, "Hmm…that was nice. Thank you for your insightful comments. I'm glad you are accompanying us."

He smiled. "I am enjoying them…and learning a lot."

Returning her gaze to her mother, Eliza apologized. "I have an appointment soon so I did not prepare lunch. I hope you have something at home."

Mrs. Claus smiled. "I do, Dear. Be sure you eat something."

"I will," Eliza assured her just before Santa transported them back to the North Pole.

She hurriedly grabbed something to eat, let the dogs outside, and changed her outfit. Stopping to initiate her circular-pattern-energy-detector, she kissed the dogs good-bye. "See you soon. I'm remembering my detector."

Transporting into the alley behind J's store, Eliza arrived a couple minutes early for their meeting. As Eliza walked into J's office, her brow furrowed. "Are you alright?" J asked. "You look stressed."

She's probably picking up my red energy, Eliza thought. "I'm fine," Eliza replied aloud. "I've had a lot going on." Attempting to divert the conversation from her, Eliza excitedly asked, "How did your friends react to Fiona's threads?"

J chuckled. "To put it mildly, they went crazy over them." She lifted a wad of papers. "I tentatively have a bunch of orders."

"Why tentatively? Do you need adjustment on them?" Eliza wondered.

"You **are** off! I can't believe you are not realizing that we didn't finalize any parts of my agreement with Fiona. You just left samples of the threads with me."

Eliza smiled. "You're right. I certainly am off." She sighed. "Do you mind if I contact Fiona? Perhaps she can transport here, and we can work this out right now."

"Fine with me. I'd love to get these orders processed today."

Eliza telepathically reached Fiona. *I'm in J's office. Can you take a few minutes right now to join us? J has orders for your threads.*

Following Eliza's coordinates, Fiona immediately appeared. She gave Eliza a double-take. "What's wrong with you?" she wondered.

Eliza chuckled. "You and J! I'm just tired. I've had a lot going on." Turning to J, Eliza encouraged, "Take it from here. I'm relaxing and listening."

After J laid out her friends' reactions, their orders, and her suggestions, she and Fiona had a back and forth finalizing the details of how J would handle selling and distributing Fiona's threads, Fiona's production particulars, and the projected delivery date for the orders. By the time they finished, Eliza had dozed off.

Smirking at J, Fiona stepped close to Eliza and

whispered in her ear, "I'm glad we lulled you to sleep. We're done."

Eliza shook herself awake. "I'm sorry. While I'm sure you didn't need me, I apologize for not being any help."

"You're right, we didn't, did we Fiona?"

"We're good." Fiona looked first at J and then at Eliza. "Thank you both for your enthusiasm over my threads. I hadn't dreamed of getting them in the human dimension. I am very excited over this venture, especially with your help."

Standing, Eliza extended her hand to shake J's. "Yes, thank you, J, for your enthusiasm and the nap. You have a nice chair."

Smiling, J replied, "I'm glad I could make you comfortable."

Eliza transported home. Fiona returned to her shop. She instantly contacted Lugh, telling him all about what just happened. She ended, "I'm worried about Eliza. She didn't look good."

"In what way?" Lugh wondered, concerned.

"Um…I'm not certain how to describe her. Not her usual self is the best I can say."

"I wonder if Santa has seen her recently?" Lugh responded. "I'll contact him."

"That's a good idea," Fiona agreed. "See you in three hours."

Santa filled Lugh in on Roger, Mittka, and Navva.

"Wow!" Lugh exclaimed when Santa finished. "No wonder she doesn't look good. One of those would be enough, but all three and at once! Do you think your supposition about her exacerbating the red energy is correct?"

"I'm not certain. We're keeping a close eye on her. Anything you and Fiona can do to help would be appreciated," Santa requested.

"We will. You know that. We love Eliza dearly. I'm so sorry she is having this experience."

"So are we, Lugh. So are we," Santa concluded.

By the time Eliza got home, she felt the exhaustion J and Fiona had seen. Suspecting Mittka either had been there or was waiting for her, she kept her circular-pattern-energy-detector active. Sliding the sunroom door open, Dusty and Chance immediately dashed down the hall to Eliza's office door, not even stopping for a hello kiss. Their actions spoke volumes and echoed what her detector was screaming. Mittka was in the room.

Hesitating before she turned the door knob, Eliza bent down and kissed each dog on the head. Swinging the door wide, she stepped into the room with a bright smile. "I see—"

Her positivity encountered a negative scowl on Mittka's face. "Are you avoiding me?" he wondered accusatorily.

She had never heard that tone from him and was surprised. He always was upbeat and pleasant. Her reply sounded defensive. "No, I had an appointment—"

Abruptly he stood, stepped over to her, and shoved her up against the wall, pinning her tightly with his body. Roughly covering her lips with his, he seemed determined to drink in her essence. She marveled that he could kiss her that long without coming up for breath. Finally, he withdrew his mouth from hers slightly, just enough to breathe for literally a couple of seconds. "Oh, that's better," he managed to whisper before returning his lips to hers.

Repeating his first effort a second time, he removed his mouth and uttered a longer comment, "I didn't think I could wait another minute for you to show up. One more time—" He interrupted his own speech, urgently locking onto Eliza's lips.

After another equally long third kiss, Eliza felt Mittka's body relax. He released his grip on her and stepped back. "There! I'm refreshed."

Gently pulling her close, he seemed more himself. "I think that will last me a couple of days. Thank you." With one more quick kiss, he disappeared.

Drained, Eliza lowered herself into the chair where Mittka had been sitting and contacted Santa. *Dad, would you please come to my office?*

He appeared in a heartbeat. His brow furrowed. "What's wrong?"

"I don't know. I feel unsteady. Would you help me lie down?"

He did. Then she weakly related her interaction with Mittka. Worried, he summoned Teeny Tiny Elf. "Would you please stay with Eliza tonight? Let me know immediately if she feels worse. I don't want to alert Navva. Do not mention this to him, okay?"

"Okay, Santa." He snuggled into Eliza's elbow. "We'll take a nap."

"I'll be back to check on her after Mrs. Claus and I go to bed."

When he returned home, he shared with Mrs. Claus what had just happened. "We'll both check on her after dinner," Mrs. Claus corrected.

Shocked at Eliza's pale and weak appearance a few hours later, Mrs. Claus exclaimed, "You didn't look this way this morning. What happened?"

"I don't know. At my appointment with J, both she and Fiona commented that I didn't look right. When I got home, I felt what they saw."

"After your interaction with Mittka?" her mother wondered.

"No, exhaustion hit me when I arrived home, before I realized he waited in my office." She sighed. "I think Roger's attack, Navva's upset, and Mittka's demands in combination are weighing me down."

"I'm the right one to help you feel better," Teeny Tiny Elf chirped. "Good thing you brought me here, Santa!"

Santa, Mrs. Claus, and Eliza chuckled. "Yes," Eliza agreed. "He makes me feel much better. Would you stay until the next interview?"

"I don't want to miss visiting Nona," he disclosed. "Santa and Mrs. Claus are planning to go tomorrow. Are you coming along?"

Mrs. Claus interrupted, "We won't go until we know Eliza is alright." She paused. "You might want to come along, too, Dear."

"Let's check on Eliza in the morning before we finalize anything," Santa stated.

Mrs. Claus slipped a container out of the bag beside her. "We brought a bit of dinner for you two. I want you to continue resting, Eliza, and you to make sure she does, Teeny Tiny Elf."

As she opened the container, Eliza sniffed the air. "Oh, thank you, Mother. I am hungry."

"You two go home," Teeny Tiny Elf suggested. "I'll clean up when we are finished."

After giving hugs and kisses, Santa and Mrs. Claus returned to their bedroom. Upon arrival, Mrs. Claus leaned against Santa. "Our precious daughter. Nothing comes easy for her, does it?"

Chapter 21

Two days later, Eliza felt fine so Santa and Mrs. Claus decided to go to Nona. Mrs. Claus wanted to check on the children and see how the Nonas handled the concoction updates. They invited Merlin, Navva, and Eliza to accompany them. Merlin accepted their invitation immediately. Navva hung back, waiting to see what Eliza chose to do. "I have work to get done and want to keep up with the book," she replied. "Please give Anax, Anassa, Amir, Doolin, and everyone else my love."

When he heard her response, Navva declined, too. Santa looked at him suspiciously. Why did Navva base his decision on Eliza's?

"Let's go," Mrs. Claus encouraged. "One hundred children to look over each will take a while."

Uneasy, Santa joined Mrs. Claus, Teeny Tiny Elf, and Merlin in transporting to Nona. Upon their arrival, they were mobbed by children, erasing Santa's angst from his mind.

Feeling better about the lack of Mittka's morning kisses and wanting to reconnect with Eliza, Navva thought he would take the opportunity to surprise her with a visit. To give her a chance to work, he waited until the afternoon to drop by.

Eliza had a productive morning, catching up on her work completely. After lunch she planned to add updates to the book. She was startled by Mittka appearing in her kitchen as she finished eating. She had rinsed her plate off in the sink and just placed the rest of the food in the refrigerator when his hand covered hers, closing the door. Drawing her to him with a look of anticipation, he urgently pressed his lips against hers. His intensity seemed to grow and, once again, he kissed her a long time. Pulling away, he mumbled, "That's a good start…"

Not surprisingly, he sucked in a quick breath and smashed her lips with another demanding kiss.

For the third kiss, he swiveled her around and pinned her between his body and the refrigerator. When he finally drew back, he smiled. "I am almost satisfied."

Although his kisses no longer enticed Eliza, Mittka seemed oblivious to her nonchalance. Their last interaction a couple days ago had made her wary. "Okay, you had your fun. I accomplished a great deal this morning and want to get back to work."

"Wow! You are all business today."

"I stayed here to do my work and writing," she replied, "and that's what I want to do. Otherwise, I would have gone to Nona."

Flashing his most enticing smile and grabbing her hand, he suggested, "Let's take a walk first. You spent all morning at your desk. Stretch your legs before you go back."

She hesitated. Placating him might get him out of here faster, she surmised. "You're right. I would be wise to take a walk. I'll introduce you to the Little Tree."

Before stopping at the Little Tree, Eliza led Mittka down a path she had established through the woods which gave her a chance to be among the trees. They ended back in front of the house. Eliza bent down. "Little Tree, this is my new friend Mittka."

"The one that likes to kiss?"

Eliza chuckled. "Yes, that one." Glancing up at Mittka, she related the story of how she had met the Little Tree and reunited with her parents. Brushing her fingers lovingly across the Little Tree's branches, she finished, "I am grateful to have the Little Tree here where we can talk every day."

Mittka, too, hunkered down. "Nice to meet you, Little Tree. You have a fascinating history."

"I am honored to meet you, Sir. May I make a request?"

Mittka nodded. "Sure."

"I like Navva. Please don't chase him away."

"Thank you for your loyalty to Navva. I will do my best not to do that…although I am tempted."

"I know," the Little Tree replied, "which is why I am asking."

"That's up to Navva," Eliza noted, settling the matter. She stood. "I'm headed back to work. Thanks for the diversion."

Mittka gazed hungrily at her lips. Wrapping his arms around her in a firm grip, he drew her very close and mumbled in an intoxicated tone, "One more kiss before I leave."

Hoping to get rid of him quickly, she complied, throwing her arms around his neck and pressing against him. Her feigned eagerness worked. She extricated herself from the shortest of the four kisses. Stepping back, she waved, and he disappeared.

Unfortunately, about the time they approached the Little Tree, Navva materialized in Eliza's living room. Putting his finger to his lips to quiet the dogs, he tip-toed down the hall to Eliza's office where he expected to find her working. Her desk chair stood empty. "Hmm…," he mused to the dogs. "Where is Eliza?"

They led him back to the living room. Walking up to the window, they looked out at Eliza and Mittka beside the Little Tree. As those two rose and Mittka received a good-bye kiss, Navva watched. His anger skyrocketed. Eliza had cloaked a clandestine meeting with Mittka by saying she had work to do.

Navva's mind clouding with rage, he returned to her office and tenuously balanced on the edge of a chair tucked in the corner between the bookcases. When Eliza entered the house, Dusty and Chance greeted her, racing ahead of her to the office. "Yeah, I know guys, enough dillydallying. I need to get writing."

She had completely forgotten about running her circular-energy-pattern-detector. If she had thought of it, she would have dismissed the necessity of activating it to detect Navva. She never anticipated danger coming from someone she loved dearly.

Eliza was lowering herself into her desk chair when Navva spoke. "I thought you had work to do."

Momentarily brightening at his presence, she exclaimed, "Navva! When—"

She didn't finish her statement as he erupted and prowled toward her in a menacing fashion. His tone filled with fury, he launched into a tirade. "Was Mittka your work? How long has he been here? What have you two been doing? Isn't he enough for you to kiss every morning of the interviews? You must meet him in secret other times, too? How many times are those? Do you see him every single morning?" He paused, catching his breath. "Maybe he's staying over some nights! I'm suddenly feeling empathetic for poor Roger. Did you treat him the same when you were together?"

"We were never together—"

"So you say now. How can I believe anything you say? You are flaunting long kisses with Mittka in front of me. You are tearing up a marriage license with an old beau. What else have you done that I don't know?"

"Navva, you have worked yourself into a rage. Please return to the North Pole before you do something you will regret."

"I already have regrets. I regret meeting you. I regret

loving you. I regret that I can't measure up to what you want." His voice cracked.

Eliza rose, intending to step toward him and calm him. That proved to be an unwise choice. His swift action caught her off guard. She didn't even have time to react with a Taekwondo move when he struck. "I regret that I can't get you out of my mind!" he screamed as his first punch slammed her left cheek. He would never forget the gut-wrenching look of shock on her face. His second thrust connected with her right cheek. Still overflowing with rage and treating her face like a punching bag, he hit her left cheek again before she crumpled to the floor, unconscious.

He stared at her inert form. Glancing at the dogs who had backed into the hall, he transported to the North Pole. Remaining in the red fog of rage, Navva packed his stuff and left Santa and Mrs. Claus's home, appearing on the beach at the North and South Pacific Ocean Dome. Plunking down onto the warm sand, he stuck his head between his knees and took deep breaths, attempting to calm down. Quite a while later, his dad walked by. "Navva? Navva?" Rory stopped, tapping Navva on the shoulder. "Navva, is that you?"

Navva raised his head, rage mixed with shame evident on his face.

Rory's brow furrowed. He reacted to the look on Navva's face with fear. "What are you doing here? Didn't you go with Santa and Mrs. Claus to Nona?"

Navva shook his head. "I should have," he mumbled.

Rory sat down on the sand beside his son. "Why didn't you?"

"I thought I'd surprise–" He couldn't say Eliza's name. He could only see the look on her face when he punched her.

"Eliza?" Rory filled in the name. "You thought you'd surprise Eliza?"

Navva nodded.

"Did you?"

Navva began to sob. Starting small, he soon sobbed so hard his entire body shook. Rory's fear grew. His stomach tied into a knot. "What happened?"

Navva couldn't reply. He continued to sob.

"Did you two have a fight?" Rory probed, hoping to get some information.

"No," Navva whispered.

"Wouldn't she see you?" Rory offered.

Again, Navva didn't reply.

"Alright," Rory consoled. "We'll sit here together, and when you can speak, tell me what happened."

Rory waited hours for Navva to be able to talk. When he finally spoke, he managed to say, "I hit her."

"You what?!" Rory exclaimed. "You hit Eliza? Is she okay?"

Navva shook his head and started to sob again.

Rory stood, grabbed Navva by the hand, and pulled him upright. "I'm taking you home and compeling you to rest. Then I'm going to check on Eliza."

After forcing Navva to lie down in Michael's bed and putting him into Dreamland, Rory transported to Santa's, knocking on the door. Santa, Mrs. Claus, Teeny Tiny Elf, and Merlin had just arrived back, smiling and laughing from the invigorating experience they had enjoyed with the children at Nona. As Santa opened the door and saw the look on Rory's face, Santa's smile died. "I am so sorry," Rory stated sorrowfully. "I am so sorry for Navva's behavior. Is Eliza okay?"

Without responding, Santa immediately tried reaching Eliza telepathically. *Eliza, Eliza, are you okay?*

No response.

Instead he received a message from Lugh. *Santa, it's dark, and Eliza's lights are not on. We haven't seen her or the dogs this afternoon. Do you want me to check on her?*

Santa felt cold dread over his entire being. *Something's wrong. We'll be there shortly.*

"Thank you, Rory, for coming over. We just returned from Nona. Your questions prompted me to try to reach her. She did not respond. We're headed there and will let you know what we find." Closing the door, he turned and hurried to the kitchen. "That was Rory. Navva did something to Eliza. She is not responding to my message. Let's go."

As they materialized in the dark kitchen, Mrs. Claus flicked on the lights. They did not detect any sign of life. Santa called for the dogs. "Dusty? Chance? Where are you?"

"We're in here," Hector, Belinda, and Cory replied. "Hurry!"

Pressing the lights in Eliza's office, Santa, Mrs. Claus, Teeny Tiny Elf, and Merlin spotted the three brownies standing on the desk. They could see dog tails sticking out of each side. "She's on the floor," Belinda indicated.

Rounding the corner of the desk, they saw Eliza wedged between her chair and the desk. "He really hit her hard–" Hector stated.

"Three times," Cory added. "She's been out for hours."

"Oh, our poor child!" Mrs. Claus cried, breaking into tears.

Sliding the chair away, Santa bent down, slipped his hands underneath Eliza's body, and picked her up, heading to her bedroom. Gently stretching her out on the bed, he examined the swelling on her face. Mrs. Claus handed him a cold cloth. "Perhaps this will wake her."

Teeny Tiny Elf leaped onto the bed, kneeling beside Eliza, crying, and uncharacteristically staying quiet.

Seeing the lights, Lugh and Fiona had arrived. "What's wrong?" Lugh asked.

Merlin answered, "Navva struck her three times, directly in the face."

"Oh, no!" Fiona exclaimed.

Handing Santa a fresh cloth, Mrs. Claus turned away, unable to stare at Eliza's pounded tissue.

"Umm…" Eliza moaned. "Ouch." Her hand grabbed Santa's. "Dad… How bad is it?"

"I don't think you want to enter a beauty contest tomorrow," he quipped, attempting to lighten the situation. "Do you have strong pain anywhere?"

"My entire head hurts."

"I'm applying healing energy. Let me know how that feels."

After a few minutes of Santa's touch, Eliza opened her eyes. "Much better, thank you."

Remaining quiet, Teeny Tiny Elf had crept closer to her. She noticed Merlin, Fiona, and Lugh. "How did you find me?"

"We had barely returned when Rory knocked on our door, apologizing for Navva's behavior." Santa paused. "He didn't know what Navva had done." Nodding to Lugh, he added, "Lugh contacted me right after Rory appeared, saying your lights were not on and you hadn't been seen all afternoon."

Eliza sighed. "I didn't run my circular-energy-pattern -detector again. I never thought of using it to detect Navva. Mittka had already stopped by. He encouraged me to stretch my legs before he left so we walked through the woods. When we were back, I introduced him to the Little Tree. Unfortunately, Navva materialized in the house and saw Mittka give me a kiss before he left."

Mrs. Claus leaned down and gave her daughter a kiss on the cheek followed by pressing her cheek lovingly against Eliza's. "I am so sorry for this experience."

Teary-eyed, Eliza gazed into her mother's eyes. "Me, too."

Straightening, Mrs. Claus asked Santa, "May Eliza have something to eat?"

Directing a question at Eliza, Santa answered, "Are you hungry?"

Worried her head would hurt, Eliza declined to nod. "Yes, I am," she replied.

"We haven't eaten yet," Mrs. Claus informed her. "Lugh and Fiona, would you like to join us?"

Lugh looked at Fiona. "Never turn down Mrs. Claus's meals."

Fiona smiled at her husband and then Mrs. Claus. "We would love to."

Santa looked at his daughter. "Are you willing to make an attempt to go to the kitchen?"

She smiled. "Yes."

"Okay. Merlin, I will help Eliza stand. Would you flank her on one side? I'll take the other, and we'll see if we can get her to the kitchen. Eliza, keep your head straight. Do not lean on either of us. Got that?" Santa instructed.

"I do."

Mrs. Claus, Teeny Tiny Elf, Fiona, and Lugh preceded them and had already taken their seats when Santa, Eliza, and Merlin slowly entered. As Santa and Merlin carefully helped Eliza lower her body onto a chair, she smiled broadly. "Being assisted by my two favorite men makes this a red-letter day. Thank you both. Ouch!"

"What hurts?" Santa inquired immediately.

"The base of my neck."

He gently massaged the area. "That's all I'm doing right now. I want to decrease the swelling." He glanced at Mrs. Claus. "After we eat, I'm leaving for a bit. I want to meet Rory at home and let him know what happened. I'll grab a mixture to help you, Eliza, and bring it back. Before I return, I'm stopping at Grandfather and Nanna's to fill them in, too. Merlin, would you stay here with us tonight so that we can keep an eye on Eliza?"

"I was about to volunteer," Merlin responded.

"Would you like our help, too?" Lugh offered.

"If you'd at least stay until I return, we would appreciate your help. We can further assess Eliza at that point." He addressed Fiona. "Welcome to the neighborhood, Fiona. If Lugh hasn't yet informed you, you are about to discover these woods have a great deal of activity."

Sitting beside Eliza on the left, Fiona placed her hand comfortingly over Eliza's. With tears in her eyes, she expressed, "I echo your mother's words. I am so sorry this happened. We are willing to do everything we can to help."

Eliza smiled. "Thank you, good neighbor." She noticed the dogs' absence. "Where are Dusty and Chance?"

"That's right!" Lugh exclaimed. "I figured they needed to go outside so I let them out and called Barney. I'll get them."

They heard his footsteps hurry down the hall, and the flurry of paws tearing to the kitchen.

Dusty and Chance settled down on either side of Eliza as if to protect her. Sitting beside Eliza on the right, Santa wondered, "Are you up to telling us specifically what happened between you and Navva?"

"I think so. I apologize in advance for emotional outbursts." She paused. "I thought I heard Hector, Cory, and Belinda trying to roust me once."

"They directed us to you when we arrived," Merlin stated.

All three appeared. "Thank you, my wonderful friends," Eliza gushed. "I appreciate you."

"We're glad you woke up," Cory noted. "Your non-responsiveness frightened us."

"We couldn't believe our screams did not wake you," Hector added.

"We even had the dogs give you a face wash. Nothing worked." Belinda finished.

"Good idea. That usually does," Eliza concurred. Taking a shaky breath, she began, "When I walked back into the house, I didn't realize Navva was here. In retrospect, Dusty and Chance tried to tell me by running down the hall in front of me to my office." She continued with the entire episode, having to pause several times when she described Navva's punching her.

Whether it was physical or emotional, her telling seemed to prompt a dizzy spell. She closed her eyes against it and gripped both Santa and Fiona's hands tightly. "Oh…."

"What is it?" Santa worriedly wondered.

"Dizzy spell…"

Mrs. Claus set a small plate of delicious-smelling food in front of Eliza. Without moving, Eliza opened her eyes, breathed in the aromas deeply, and smiled. "You're right, Lugh, Mother's food is not to be missed."

Fiona stood. "Let me help you eat." Picking up a fork, she guided food into Eliza's mouth at a comfortable pace. When the plate was empty, Eliza commented, "As usual, that was scrumptious, Mother, and just the right amount. Thank you for your help, Fiona."

"Is the dizzy spell past?" Santa questioned.

"I think so."

He glanced at everyone around the table. "I'm leaving. I'll make my absence brief. Would you all sit here until I return? I think staying here for a bit would be good for Eliza. Teeny Tiny Elf, Merlin, and Mrs. Claus, tell about our day. I'm certain everyone would like to hear about it. If Eliza has another dizzy spell, summon me immediately."

Chapter 22

Giving Eliza a kiss on the cheek, Santa disappeared. En route to home, he telepathically asked Rory to meet him in Mrs. Claus's kitchen. They arrived simultaneously. "Pull up a chair," Santa invited.

Once Rory had taken a seat, Santa began, "Thank you for alerting us. Eliza was lying unconscious on the floor of her office. Navva had punched her in the face three times."

Rory gasped. "What precipitated that?"

Santa detailed today's incident and some of the others he and Eliza had noticed lately.

"Will she be alright from Navva's punches?" Rory wondered.

"I think so," Santa assured. "She has some dizziness and lots of swelling, which, considering the blows she absorbed, is to be expected."

Rory bent his head. When he raised it, he stuttered, "I-I-I don't know where to begin. I am ashamed of Navva's actions. I am deeply sorry for Eliza's injuries." He shook his head. "I don't know what to do."

"Give Navva your love and support," Santa suggested.

"Do you mean condone his actions?" Rory replied, horrified.

"No," Santa clarified, "but don't reprimand him for them. He is doing enough of that himself, I'm certain." He paused. "Navva has some intense emotional issues from Teacher's upbringing. He can only be fixed if he decides to be. Nudge him carefully in that direction, but let him make the decision."

"Who can help him? You can't," Rory noted.

"You're right. I can't and neither can you or Maria or Mrs. Claus for that matter. Grandfather and Nanna can, but, again, allow him to think of them and make the contact. I cannot emphasize enough that this must be his decision." Santa halted, knowing an unpleasant scenario needed to be voiced. "Watch him closely. He may be suicidal."

"That has crossed my mind in the last few seconds," Rory agreed. "I will." Standing, he enveloped Santa in a tight embrace. "Thank you, my good friend, for your candor and advice. I appreciate your lack of recrimination."

"We all love Navva and want to have him healed. Eliza would be the first to say that his physical blows today scream 'Help me!'"

As Rory transported to Violet and Scott's, Santa found the mixture he wanted and telepathically announced to Grandfather and Nanna that he was on his way to their place. Nanna had tea and dessert from dinner on the table when Santa appeared. "Eliza's premonition came true today," he began and related the day's happenings.

Nanna and Grandfather's looks morphed from alarm to concern to puzzlement. When Santa finished, Grandfather asked, "Is Eliza okay?"

"She had a dizzy spell before I left, but I haven't heard she's had another. From what I've seen, I think she will be." He smiled ruefully. "She's pretty tough."

"She is your and Mrs. Claus's child," Nanna pointed out. "That alone gives her more toughness than the average wizard."

"Is Navva being watched?" Grandfather wondered, sharing Santa's concern about suicide.

"Rory is doing that," Santa replied and repeated the conversation the two of them just finished.

"How do we fix Navva?" Nanna questioned.

"If he comes to you, you will figure out what to do. Of that I am certain. He needs your objectivity and love," Santa explained.

"Those are exactly the two words your daughter used," Grandfather noted.

Santa smiled. "She's right."

Nanna placed her hand lovingly over Santa's. "Please give Eliza our love and concern for her health and recovery from this awful experience."

"At least she survived it," Grandfather added.

"That's precisely what has gone through my head," Santa agreed. "That red energy she has around her is wreaking havoc for her. She's still in danger and not necessarily from Navva."

"Impress that upon her," Grandfather cautioned.

"I already have begun," Santa reported, "and will do more. For her protection, she needs to be super alert."

Giving Rebel, who had settled beside Santa's chair, several strokes, Santa addressed him, "I'll extend love to her from all of you." Glancing at Grandfather and Nanna, he offered, "I'd better get back to Eliza's."

"Keep in touch about Navva and Eliza," Grandfather requested.

Santa's nod was their last image of him before he disappeared in transport.

"From your telling, sounds like the children are all doing well and the Nonas are thriving," summarized Lugh. Those were the words Santa heard as he materialized back at Eliza's.

Merlin nodded. "That's correct. All four of us were invigorated by the visit."

Without interrupting the conversation, Santa began applying his mixture to Eliza's neck and shoulders.

"How is your concoction working, Mrs. Claus?" Fiona wondered.

"Very well. The elves and fairies at the domes have latched onto this challenge and are thrilled by the results. Their slowly adding more plant substance to the concoction is increasing the nourishment Nonas receive in the right amounts. Nonas have not experienced any discomfort imbibing each new version."

"Wow! That is very satisfying for the dome staff, Mom," Eliza inserted. Forgetting Santa's instruction not to move her head, Eliza turned to face her dad now seated beside her. "I feel your mixture penetrating my tissues, Dad. I am receiving a lot of relief. Thanks."

He smiled. "Good."

"How did Rory handle your news?" Mrs. Claus wondered.

"He was shocked and sends his apologies, Eliza," Santa began and related both visits.

When he finished, Eliza sighed. "I hope Navva seeks out Grandfather and Nanna."

"We do, too," Lugh echoed.

"Sounds like you had an interesting conversation while I was gone," Santa noted. "Eliza, let's give you a chance to rest. Merlin, would you repeat helping me assist her to lie down?" Glancing around, he added, "I would like someone to be in the bedroom with her all night, in case she has a dizzy spell or a great deal of discomfort. Lugh and Fiona, would you stay and take the first two-hour shift?"

Looking at his wife for approval, Lugh responded, "Sure. We'll go home after, sleep in our own bed, and return for breakfast. Is that okay with you, Fiona?"

She smirked at Mrs. Claus. "He wants another excuse to enjoy your cooking. I don't blame him. I loved this delicious meal. Thank you."

"I'll take the second shift," Merlin volunteered.

"I'll handle the third," Santa offered. "Mrs. Claus can made breakfast when she finishes hers."

Finally finding his voice, Teeny Tiny Elf crawled into Eliza's lap. "I'll stay with you all night. Is that okay, Eliza?"

She smiled and hugged him. "Sure."

"I'm sorry I left you today. I ought to have stayed. I could have stopped Navva from hitting you."

Tears trickled down her face. "I don't think you could have done that," she replied in a sad voice. "You would not have recognized him. I didn't. He was so angry."

Teeny Tiny Elf leaned against her and muffled into her chest, "I'm just glad you're alive."

When Merlin pulled up a chair to sit next to the bed for his shift, Eliza awoke. She had slept during Lugh and Fiona's shift but felt restless. She placed her hand on his. "Hi."

He smiled in relief. "Hi. You never cease to amaze me. You are handling what you experienced today with calm and concern for Navva."

"I love him, Merlin."

"I understand. Your concern differs from that of most I have encountered in your situation."

"How?"

"You are not focused on him returning to you but that he fixes himself for his sake. Your love is selfless." He paused. "Of course, that is a hallmark of your parents, too, selfless love."

She smiled ruefully. "I'm not an easy person have as a permanent partner."

"Is that why he hasn't proposed?"

"We haven't known each other long enough for a proposal."

"You think time makes a difference?"

She chuckled. "Discussing this subject with you exposes the weaknesses in my arguments."

"The ones you have had in your head as to his lack of a proposal?"

"Yes, those."

"Are they why you went to The Healing Place?"

"Yes." Eliza paused. "Ironic, isn't it? The instant I met Navva I wanted to be with him for the rest of my life. As he has witnessed my abilities, he has been stunned."

"But he hasn't shied away..." Merlin emphasized.

Eliza sighed. "No, but his contrasting my abilities with his contributes to his feelings of inadequacy."

"Have you come to grips with him not being your permanent partner?"

"I think so. Powerful wizards are a challenge to be around. If Dad did not have Mother, I strongly suspect he might be alone. You are a important mentor to me, and I console myself that you deal well with being alone."

Merlin appeared wistful. "I've had my chances, and I fully understand your point." He hesitated. "You see yourself as a powerful wizard?"

"I'd be lying if I didn't admit I see my abilities," Eliza replied, "and they appear to be increasing."

"You're right." He halted. "If you woke up, I had another subject I wanted to discuss with you."

"What's that?"

"One that involves being a powerful wizard. As a baby, you were exposed to the red energy in which Pan is immersed. A bit of that energy has stuck with you – for whatever reason. I don't think he intended it. He wanted you to die so applying a dangerous energy to affect you in the future had not been his aim."

"Why do you call red energy dangerous? I thought red represented energy."

"That's true. Remember red energy is the most densely packed and slowest moving of all energy?"

"Um hum."

"When red energy is around a being that is of reproductive age, the energy acquires the drive to have children due to its association with the sacral chakra. That prompts the red energy to want to pick up speed, generating anger and frustration at the being itself and others. Densely packed energy attempting to go faster is unsettling, confusing, and disrupting."

"Okay…"

"Powerful wizards exacerbate the energies around them–"

"Thus, red energy around you, me, or Dad will be heightened, creating danger for the wizard," Eliza finished.

Merlin nodded. "Exactly. I've only seen this in males. You are the first powerful female wizard I've known. I can cite examples of how males have dealt with it. I suspect differences exist."

"In what way?"

"If rebuffed, females tend to give up more easily than males. As Roger demonstrated, males will doggedly return."

"Is males' drive stronger?" Eliza questioned.

"Perhaps. Or, perhaps their attitude that perseverance wins the day keeps them in the fray."

"So you are telling me that as a female you suspect I will have more difficulty with the red energy than you or Dad would?"

"Yes."

"What difference does that make?" she wondered.

"You need to be hyper alert for signs of it and be prepared to control the situation."

Santa strolled into the room. "Thank you, Merlin. I couldn't sleep worrying about Eliza, and I have listened to much of your conversation. You helped me a great deal and likely explained the red energy better than I would have done."

"You are welcome." He glanced at Eliza. "Your captivating beauty draws attention to you, too."

"As I review my interaction with Navva, once he entred my office I had three options: Taekwondo, a bolt, or a freeze, right?"

"And cornered beside your desk, most of those ceased to be viable options," Merlin noted.

"That's why you must always be running your circular-pattern-energy-detector," Santa advised. "You want to know immediately that you have encountered a problem so that you have the most feasible options of what to do."

"Would you go over the options with me?"

"I will," Santa replied.

"That's a excellent idea," Merlin concurred.

"We'll start tomorrow if you feel better," Santa finalized, wanting to school her as soon as possible before she encountered another incident.

She smiled weakly. "That sounds good," she mumbled, closing her eyes.

Out of an abundance of caution, Merlin and Santa once again helped Eliza to the kitchen for breakfast. Fiona and Lugh had already taken their seats. "How are you feeling?" Lugh asked anxiously.

As Santa and Merlin lowered her into the chair, she smiled and winked. "With this much attention, I might be out of sorts for a while." She broke into a laugh. "Thank you, Dad and Merlin. I love your help."

Addressing Lugh's question, she added, "I am still sore but able to move my head almost normally, thanks to Dad's mixture and healing touch."

Suddenly Violet and Scott materialized. They hurried over to Eliza. "Rory just told us what happened," Violet exclaimed. "Are you okay?"

Before Eliza could answer, Scott inquired of Santa, "What's your prognosis?"

"She'll be fine." Santa chuckled. "Her hard head has once again stood her in good stead."

Eliza grabbed her dad's hand, returning the quip. "I come from hard-headed stock."

"Pull up a chair and have breakfast with us, Mom and Dad," Mrs. Claus invited.

"Thank you," Violet replied, "but we'd better get home. Navva is about to wake up, and we are worried about what Maria will say to him. She already responded inappropriately to Rory's telling of what happened."

Eliza looked sadly at Violet. "She likely stated I brought this on with my kissing of Mittka." Eliza paused. "And, that I deserved it for my actions."

Violet was silent, but Scott agreed. "That is exactly what she foolishly uttered."

"Right now, Maria is Navva's biggest impediment to getting better," Mrs. Claus stated. "Please do everything you can to mitigate the impact of her words on him."

"We will," Violet assured her daughter.

After giving Eliza a kiss, they disappeared back to the North Pole.

Chapter 23

Navva slowly regained consciousness. He looked around. He didn't recognize his surroundings. Where was he? Abruptly the full realization of what he had done surfaced. He saw the horror on Eliza's face as he'd struck her. Why had he done that? How could he slug the woman he loved? What drove him to hurt the person who had treated him with the most kindness of anyone he had met?

He rolled over, buried his head in the pillow and sobbed uncontrollable, gut-wrenching gasps. What could she possibly have done to deserve that treatment, especially from him?

A voice in his head answered. *She kissed Mittka.*

In defense of her, he responded, *So what? Was a kiss or two or however many deserving of that punishment?*

Teacher would say so.

Teacher?! He mentally screamed. *Could he never be rid of that awful individual?*

He returned to lying on his back. There's one way to be rid of him, Navva thought. I can get him out of my head permanently if I no longer think.

Someone softly opened the door to the room. "Naava?" whispered Rory. "Navva? Are you awake?"

He didn't want to be. Navva didn't want to face his father. He didn't want to face Mrs. Claus. He didn't want to face–

Rory softly walked over to the bed, settling down on the side. He noticed Navva's wet face. "I'm sorry for your pain, Son."

"How could I do that, Dad?" Navva barely uttered. "Why would I be so enraged I would hurt–" He swallowed hard. He couldn't say Eliza's name out loud. Finally he blurted, "her?"

Rory shook his head. "I don't know, Son. I don't know."

Sobs welled up in Navva. "Why do you want to acknowledge that I'm your son after what I did?"

"Because I love you."

A paralyzing question flashed into Navva's mind. For a few seconds he vacillated between voicing it and not, uncertain if he wanted to know the answer. The torture of not knowing finally drove him to eke out, "Is she alive?"

Navva felt the seconds between when he asked and his dad answered stretch out interminably long. Finally, Rory nodded, "Yes."

Navva released the deepest sigh Rory had ever heard.

Attempting to divert the subject, Rory suggested, "I know your answer will be to decline my offer, but please don't. If I bring some breakfast in here, would you please eat?"

Navva stared at his dad. He didn't feel hungry. *You need sustenance,* his body elemental noted.

Is food worth my time?

Yes.

Amazing Rory three minutes later, Navva replied. "Okay."

"I'll be right back," Rory responded.

Before Navva could change his mind, Rory stepped outside the door and received a tray from Violet. "Thanks," he murmured as he accepted it.

Rory stayed with Navva as he ate, making certain he finished as much as possible. Surprising both, Navva cleaned his plate. "My body elemental advised me to eat. I didn't realize I was this hungry."

Setting the tray on the floor, Rory leaned toward his son, giving him a kiss on the cheek. "I'm putting you in Dreamland. You can help yourself the most with rest."

Not able to muster a smile, Navva stared into his father's eyes with a wounded look. "Thanks, Dad."

Sliding back down, Navva adjusted his neck into a comfortable position. As Rory brushed his hand across his son's forehead, Navva closed his eyes, welcoming the escape from his thoughts to Dreamland.

About the same time, Patrick and Robin appeared in Eliza's kitchen. Mrs. Claus and Teeny Tiny Elf had just cleared all the breakfast dishes off the table. They both addressed Eliza. "How are you?"

Grabbing her dad's hand and wincing as she did, she replied, "I may not look the best, and I've definitely felt better, but Dad's healing touch has worked miracles on me."

Their gaze shifted to Santa. "As you requested, we moved today's interview to two days from now," Patrick informed.

"We also confirmed the final interview for the original date of the following day," Robin added.

"Thank you," Santa replied. "Eliza will be able to handle the interview in two days and another the day after. In light of the present situation, I think finishing on that date is wise."

"What was Mittka's response?" Merlin wondered.

"He didn't seem to have a reaction," Robin noted. "He said, 'Okay.' Nothing else."

"Hmm…," Merlin mumbled.

"We would appreciate everyone here keeping the incident among this group," Mrs. Claus requested. "Navva needs help. We don't want versions of what happened coming at him."

"We all love Navva," Lugh remarked, "and want him to heal. We won't contribute any impediment to that happening."

Everyone murmured agreement.

Merlin turned toward Eliza. "Prior to yesterday, when was the last time Mittka sought out your kisses?"

Through her hazy thoughts Eliza found her answer. "Two days before."

"After Patrick and Robin lengthened the interval between excursions," Santa noted, "Mittka went five days without getting a kiss. He received the next three days later."

"Morning or afternoon?" Merlin asked Eliza.

"Afternoon."

"Did you say he was surly?"

Eliza nodded. "Uncharacteristically so."

Merlin halted, computing. "Expect him to visit you tomorrow morning."

"Why do you say that?"

"His obsession is increasing, and he needs a dose of you more frequently. I surmise he became surly waiting for you two days ago."

"He accused me of avoiding him."

As if agreeing with his assessment, Merlin nodded. "The further he goes into the second day, the more anxious he becomes. In order to reduce his anxiety, he will appear earlier."

Merlin, Santa, and Mrs. Claus exchanged looks. "Teeny Tiny Elf, you stay with Eliza the next few days, okay?" Mrs. Claus suggested.

"Gladly. What do you want me to do?" Teeny Tiny Elf asked.

"Help divert Mittka's angst," Merlin noted. "Ask him for a kiss on the cheek. Act normally and be yourself. Follow the impulses that come to you in the moment."

Santa agreed. Turning to Eliza, he added, "Despite being anxious, he was friendly, right?"

"Um hum."

"As we discussed, maintain boundaries but accommodate him within those limits. If he is amenable, be agreeable to his wishes," Santa advised.

"Like four kisses?"

Santa waved his hand. "Whatever. Keep your interaction friendly. Although I'm certain you can handle him, don't invite an altercation."

"I'm not interested in that, either."

"I know you're not," Santa concurred, "but do your very best not to prompt him to it. I have a feeling it's coming. I would like to stave it off as long as possible, giving Merlin, your mother, and me a chance to mull over our options of how to address this situation."

"If you think I could be helpful," Fiona offered, "I'll stay home the next few days. Lugh and I will keep an eye on activity here, just in case we can interrupt in a helpful way."

"Thank you, Fiona," Santa expressed. "That is a very good idea. The two of you could work in the yard or do something outside which appears normal but actually distracts Mittka's attention."

Their planning turned out to be fortuitous.

Merlin's prediction came true the next morning just after Eliza and Teeny Tiny Elf had finished breakfast and cleaned up. "I'll take Dusty and Chance outside," he offered. "We'll play with Barney for a while."

"See you soon," Eliza replied, heading down the hall to her office.

She opened the door and Mittka appeared simultaneously. Attempting to cover his urgent desire with pleasantries, he slid his arm around Eliza's waist and drew her close. "Oh," he breathed, "Your scent is wonderful."

"I have a new soap," she replied, wondering how long he could maintain small talk.

No longer. He bent toward her and covered her lips with his, much more gently than two days ago. Although his desire did not seem acute, he continued the kiss a long time. When he raised his lips slightly away from hers, he was breathing heavily. Eliza had the distinct impression his craving was intensifying.

She was right. He pushed her against the closed door, pinning her and once again claiming her lips with his. As his kiss lengthened, he seemed to want her even closer, using his hands on her back to press her into his chest.

Having difficulty breathing, she was grateful when he pulled both his lips and body away from hers so that she could breathe normally. "I am intoxicated by you more and more," Mittka passionately whispered. "How do you do this to me?"

Eliza smiled. "I have more power than you realize."

They heard a commotion in the hall. The door slammed, and Teeny Tiny Elf yelled, "That was fun! Eliza, where are you?"

"In my office," she responded, maintaining her smile. "Mittka's here."

Pushing on the door, he ordered, "Let me in. I want a kiss from Mittka."

Mittka backed off, allowing Eliza to open the door. Glancing at her, Teeny Tiny Elf noticed her puffy, bruised lips. He leaped into Mittka's arms and presented his right cheek. Pointing, he indicated, "Put it right there, please."

As Mittka did, Teeny Tiny Elf oozed, "Mmm, that is nice!"

"What are you doing here?" Mittka wondered.

"Every once in a while, I like to stay with Eliza. I get to see her, play with Dusty and Chance, and visit my cousin Eddie."

"How long are you here this time?" Mittka probed.

Teeny Tiny Elf shrugged. "As long as I feel like it, right, Eliza?"

She reached over and tickled him. "You never stay long enough for me."

Leaving Mittka, Teeny Tiny Elf jumped into Eliza's arms. "I'll see you tomorrow," Mittka noted. Leaning over

Teeny Tiny Elf, Mittka covered Eliza's lips one more time. The shortest of his four kisses, Mittka still seemed loathe to end it. When he did, he disappeared.

For several minutes, Eliza and Teeny Tiny Elf stood still, apprehensive about moving or saying anything for fear Mittka would reappear. He didn't. "He must be satiated," Eliza mumbled in Teeny Tiny Elf's ear. "Good job. Thank you!"

Giving her a hug and kissing her on the cheek, he smiled into her eyes. "I love you and want you safe." He paused. "Did he mention your bruises?"

"No. He's too focused on satisfying his desire."

"At least you didn't have to explain them and tell him about Navva."

"Yes, I'm thankful for that."

Mrs. Claus and Santa showed up with dinner that evening, partly to give Eliza relief from cooking and partly to check on the events of the day. She and Teeny Tiny Elf related their satisfactory handling of Mittka. When they finished, Eliza asked, "What is going on with him? Why does he feel the urgency to kiss me every forty-eight hours, as Merlin noted?"

"We speculate that you have unknowingly melded a bit of Pan's red energy that is clinging to you with other energy and are channeling the combination. We further postulate that you are unwittingly increasing the red of that blend through your power. When Mittka kisses you, he receives the powerful red blend. That appears to be addictive for him, and his addiction is prompting him to crave more and more."

"Why does he need more every forty-eight hours? Is he losing it?"

"That perplexes us," Mrs. Claus replied. "Losing it doesn't make sense. Perhaps it loses its red punch that you apply. We haven't been able to arrive at an answer."

"What we can tell," Santa added, "is that he is voracious about it."

"Is that why you suspect an altercation?"

Both her parents nodded. "His anxiety a couple days ago indicates his mood is becoming increasingly enraged about getting more, which is dangerous," Mrs. Claus explained.

"I perceive his personality is changing," Eliza remarked. "The day I met him, he seemed upbeat, fun, and friendly. His kisses that day felt exciting and enticing. Now they are not. What has changed, his kisses or me?"

"What do you think, Teeny Tiny Elf?" Mrs. Claus inquired.

"His kisses feel the same to me!" he responded.

"He hasn't kissed me lately so I cannot give my perspective," Mrs. Claus noted.

"Where does the escalation of his need end?" Eliza asked apprehensively.

Mrs. Claus addressed Santa. "Would I help by seeking his kiss tomorrow so that I can find out if it feels the same to me?"

Santa sighed. "I doubt that he will care about kissing you with Eliza nearby. He may wonder why you are requesting a kiss when you have never done that." He glanced at their daughter. "His obsession may spark wariness, and he may take particular notice of out-of-the-ordinary actions."

"So I wouldn't be smart to give him a quick kiss tomorrow morning, either, because that would be out of the ordinary with recent excursions," Eliza remarked.

"Sadly, yes," Santa concurred. "I suspect his conniving with you at another time to receive these kisses when no one else is around excites him, too."

"That's why you want Teeny Tiny Elf with me," Eliza surmised. "He is an unobtrusive distraction."

"Exactly," Santa agreed.

"Alright. I will expect Mittka to show up tomorrow afternoon and the afternoon of the next day following our final excursion." Eliza hesitated. "After two days in a row, he ought to be quite satiated. Will he want to set up a daily meeting or some way to have contact in order to continue the kisses? What do I do if he does?"

"We are worried he will want to take you with him," Mrs. Claus disclosed.

"We hope that doesn't happen," Santa countered. "We hope his satiation calms him and doesn't cause him to think about the next day."

"That's why you are concerned about an altercation," Eliza exclaimed. "You think I will resist him."

Her parents' faces gave their answer.

"What do you recommend in that situation?" Eliza wondered.

"Has he seen you shoot bolts?" Santa questioned

"No, I don't think he knows I can."

"Shoot a couple on either side of him. Those may startle him enough to back off."

"Is a freeze my next move?" Eliza suggested.

Santa nodded. "If necessary, yes, then summon me."

All four, including Teeny Tiny Elf, left the conversation with an unsettled feeling.

Chapter 24

Teeny Tiny Elf greeted Patrick and Robin the next morning. "Good morning! Eliza will be right out."

In quick succession Santa and Mrs. Claus arrived followed by Mittka and finally Eliza. Mittka's gaze instantly fixated on Eliza's lips. Everyone felt his obsession. Ignoring him, Eliza brightly asked Patrick and Robin, "What is today's topic?"

"Trees' consciousness," Robin responded. "We have two stops."

Anxious to divert Mittka's attention, Patrick nudged Santa, "I have the coordinates in mind."

Santa transported them to a woods filled with oaks, maples, and poplars. They stood on one of several paths they noticed that wound through the trees. Here and there they saw benches upon which to relax and soak in the atmosphere. They seemed to be alone with the trees at that time of day. Patrick turned to an oak beside him. "Thank you for sharing your observations with us today. I am pleased to introduce Mittka, Santa, Mrs. Claus, their daughter Eliza who is writing the book, and their family member Teeny Tiny Elf."

"Welcome to our woods," the oak returned. "You honor us with your presence."

"We are honored to meet you," Eliza replied.

"You can hear me?"

"Yes, Dad taught me to talk to trees. I find doing so fascinating and fulfilling. I love trees," Eliza explained.

"Thank you."

Patrick offered the first question, "What have you noticed about humans who seek your company?"

"We seem to have a calming effect upon them," the oak noted.

"I read a study done by scientists in Korea comparing the effect on older women of walking among the trees or in a city," Eliza began. "Near the trees, their blood pressure, lung capacity, and arterial elasticity improved. In the city none of those happened."

"That doesn't surprise me," the oak responded. "Although they do not hear us as you do, we talk to them as they stroll between us, doing our best to make them feel their best. They love to be around us and feel our presence."

"While they may not consciously hear your talk, I suspect at a certain level they recognize it," Eliza assured.

"At our Growing Grounds," Mrs. Claus inserted, "the trees instill a positivity in all who visit and work there. We have even found the plants near trees are affected by the trees' proximity and do better."

"Our slow pace is quite a contrast with the daily routine of human society," the oak remarked.

"What humans need," replied Eliza. "They are lured into going fast all the time when that is not good for them."

The oak directed a question to Santa. "How did you teach your daughter to talk to trees?"

"I encouraged her to meditate. That opened her up to hearing trees, rocks, and most parts of nature."

"With that, he opened up other dimensions for me, too," Eliza added.

"Other dimensions I understand," the oak agreed, "but you are the first wizards I have met who are willing to talk to trees, rocks, and other beings in the natural world."

"We want humans to do that through meditating," Eliza explained. "That's a big reason we are writing these books."

"How can we help you accomplish your goal?"

"Keep on talking to humans. Perhaps one day someone will reply. Continue to send them calming energy so that they seek your company," Eliza suggested.

"Some humans have epiphanies when they are around us. That is partly due to our being able to read their minds and send thoughts to help them," the oak revealed.

"Really?!" Eliza exclaimed. "You send them ideas?"

"Yes. Although that concept may shock humans, we do operate at a higher vibration than them, giving us a broader perspective," the oak explained.

Robin added, "Even tree consciousness that is not a deva vibrates at a higher frequency than humans. All trees occupy a deva position to humans."

"Give humans the message that we can help and not to think their trust in us is unusual. Most humans share that basic understanding," the oak assured them.

"Thank you. You have given me reassurance, new information, and your calming presence. I appreciate you," Eliza concluded.

"Hi, Tree, I'm Teeny Tiny Elf. I love you!" he blurted, leaping up to the lowest branch and giving the oak a hug.

"Thank you, Teeny Tiny Elf. That felt good," the oak replied.

Santa, Mrs. Claus, Mittka, Robin, and Patrick also expressed their thanks. As Mittaka stepped back to stand beside Eliza, he ran his hand up her back and gazed hungrily at her lips. She knew he wanted to pull her to him and kiss her right there. He was applying every ounce of energy to hold himself back. Plan on another visit today, she thought. I wonder how quickly he comes back after we return?

"Would you use the coordinates in my mind to take us to the second stop?" Patrick asked Santa.

Santa's eyes widened in surprise. A couple seconds later, Eliza understood why. She gasped. "My woods before the tornado!" She turned to Patrick. "Is this my woods before the tornado?"

"We thought you'd like to time travel back here and include a talk with your woods in the book."

Tears flowing down her face, Eliza spread her arms wide. "Oh, my wonderful tree friends, if I had only known that September 24 was the last I would see you, I would have said good-bye that day." She stopped, releasing a sob. "I understand the Universe does not give us warnings to do that. I am thrilled to see you again, have the chance to talk to you, and bid you good-bye. How precious!" She turned to Patrick and Robin. "Thank you both!!"

Everyone could feel a low hum. "My song that I love to sing you! What an affectionate response!" Eliza gushed.

"They encourage me to tell humans to sing to trees. They love sound, and the sound of human singing particularly catches their attention." Eliza paused. "Their noting human sound reminds me that fairies expressed the same sentiment."

She became very quiet. "Me, too," she replied. "Several commented how many times I expressed thanks for their keeping the woods cool in the summer and warm in the winter. I could literally feel a ten degree temperature difference when I entered and shared my appreciation out loud."

Eliza nodded. "They tell me that I spoke to them a lot and thanked them a lot. That's true." She chuckled. "They mention Dusty and Chance and the dogs' playfulness."

She began to sob. Mrs. Claus wrapped her arm around Eliza comfortingly. When Eliza could talk, she bid her friends good-bye. "I'm having Dad teach me how to time travel just so I can come back and see you again. So, this will not be good-bye. I am extending more thanks.

Thanks for being part of my life and allowing me to live with you. You overwhelm me."

Remaining quiet for a few seconds, Eliza gave Patrick and Robin the sign that she was ready to leave. She continued to send love even during transport. When they arrived in her kitchen, she threw her arms around Santa. "Thanks, Dad!"

He held her tightly, knowing how much seeing the trees meant to her.

Unable to control himself, Mittka abruptly disappeared without saying good-bye. In an anxious state, he could feel himself rapidly worsening. He needed Eliza's kiss soon.

Santa and Mrs. Claus thanked Patrick and Robin. They bid the four good-bye. "See you tomorrow!" Robin finished.

"We'll bring dinner later," Mrs. Claus softly remarked before they transported.

Leaping into Eliza's arms, Teeny Tiny Elf whispered, "I think you will have a visitor in your office any second." Hopping off her arm and tearing down the hall, he exclaimed in his regular voice, "I'll go outside for a few minutes with Dusty and Chance. See you shortly!"

Thinking today that her office was the wisest move, Eliza walked down the hall to it at a normal pace. Opening the door, she felt it ripped out of her fingers and slammed shut. She was pushed up against it. Before her back touched the door, Mittka's mouth enveloped hers in a hard kiss. He held her in that position so long she thought she would pass out from lack of breath. About the time she felt light-headed, he just barely lifted his lips.

Releasing three deep breaths in quick succession, he again engulfed her mouth without saying a word. Knowing his pattern and recognizing he would take more, Eliza had sucked in three quick, deep breaths, hoping that would hold her through his second kiss. She navigated the second one better than the first.

He pulled away a little further the second time. "I didn't think I could last," he breathed.

Seeming to come to life, he gazed passionately at her lips. "One more, okay?" he mumbled. "I know Teeny Tiny Elf will be back any minute."

Without waiting for her response, he kissed her a third and final time, disappearing when he was done. Eliza heard the back door open and the flurry of paws and elfin feet headed her way.

Breathing hard, Eliza lowered herself into the chair Navva had used between the bookcases. When Teeny Tiny Elf threw the door open, he became alarmed. He didn't see her. "Eliza!" he screamed. "Eliza! Where are you?"

Desperately afraid Mittka had kidnapped her, he quieted, thinking he heard something. Peeking around the door, he spied Eliza sitting, unable to talk for lack of breath. He jumped into her arms and leaned against her. "You scared me! I couldn't see you and was petrified Mittka had taken you away."

They sat in that position for a bit, Eliza working to return her breathing to normal, and Teeny Tiny Elf cuddling close to her chest. Hugging him to her, Eliza stood, walked to the kitchen, and placed him in a chair. "I'll make lunch. Thank you for being here. He left in anticipation of your return with the dogs."

"Whew! That was close," he exclaimed. "I had a very bad feeling he had kidnapped you."

Eliza shook her head. "If not for his weakened state, I think he might have." She paused. "Tomorrow we are headed outside beside the Little Tree after we return. I want space to handle him."

"Let's talk to Santa and Mrs. Claus about that tonight," he suggested.

"We will."

Thankful that Navva had eaten every meal for the last two days, Rory attempted to have a conversation with his son. Although Navva had been willing to eat, he would not leave the bedroom. He had kept the bedroom door between him and the world, consuming his meals in the room and forcing his dad to come there to speak with him.

Navva refused to talk with anyone except Rory. Without any knowledge of how to handle someone in Navva's state, Rory felt ill-equipped to find the right words for what he wanted to say. He decided to project love and tip-toe through the interaction carefully. Rory began with a compliment, "I'm glad you have been eating. Thank you."

With a solemn face, Navva accepted his dad's gratitude. "You are welcome."

"How are you feeling?" Rory wondered.

Navva shrugged. "Okay." He paused. "Do you mean about what I did? Rotten. I feel horrible. Over and over I keep asking myself why I did it. I cannot come up with an answer."

"Do you love her?" Rory avoided using Eliza's name since Navva had yet to speak it.

Navva scoffed. "Are you joking? Of course! Yes, I love her completely, with all my heart."

"Did you see yourself spending your life with her?"

Tears trickled out of Navva's eyes and flowed down his cheeks. "I did. I doubt that's possible anymore."

"Why do you say that?" Rory probed.

"Because I slugged her, Dad!" Navva replied in an exasperated, raised voice. "Would you spend your life with someone who slugged you? Wouldn't you be wondering when he might do it again?"

"I don't know. I've never been hit by someone I love," Rory admitted.

"Rub it in."

"I'm sorry," Rory apologized. "I did not intend that. I'm being truthful."

"I never thought I'd beat up anyone, especially someone I love," Navva confessed.

Although he knew the answer, Rory asked the next question innocently, "What precipitated your anger?"

Navva hesitated, shook his head, and cried. Rory had just about given up receiving an answer when Navva quietly replied, "She was kissing Mittka."

"Did that surprise you?"

"Well, no. She had kissed him every time we met to go on the first few excursions."

"Regularly?" Rory questioned.

"Yeah. I guess he likes to kiss, especially women."

"Did he kiss other women?"

Navva held off replying. Finally, he nodded. "He kissed Mrs. Claus."

Rory reacted swiftly. "In front of Santa?"

"Yes," Navva acknowledged.

"What did Santa say?"

"Something about that if she liked to enjoy perfection, he didn't mind."

Rory stifled a chuckle. That sounded exactly like a comment Santa would make. He and Mrs. Claus enjoyed a well-founded, stable relationship. "Did you ask yourself why Mittka kissing her bothered you when Mrs. Claus kissing him didn't affect Santa?"

Navva blurted, "He liked kissing her more that he liked kissing Mrs. Claus. He did it more. Then I saw him kissing her at her house with no one but them around. I wondered how often they had been doing that behind my back."

"Behind your back?"

"Yeah."

Their discussion had been open and frank. Rory didn't want to interrupt the flow, but he felt compelled to ask, "What claim do you have on her?"

Navva's brow furrowed. "What do you mean?"

"Do you have an agreement only to see each other? Have you discussed spending your lives together? Have you proposed?"

Navva did not reply. For a long time he sat silent. Rory waited, not willing to let this drop. In his view, Navva needed to acknowledge and answer this point. Finally, Navva mumbled, "No."

"No to which one?" Rory pressed.

"No to all."

Feeling defensive, Navva added, "She helped rescue me and nurse me back to health after Teacher tried to kill me. I've been staying with Santa and Mrs. Claus in her bedroom. She greets me with a loving kiss. I assumed—"

Following his instinct that he had control of the conversation, Rory interrupted, "You assumed. Assuming always gets you in trouble."

Signaling their conversation had ended, Rory stood. "Think about it."

He leaned down and gave Navva a kiss on the cheek. "Good night. See you in the morning."

Chapter 25

That evening Santa and Mrs. Claus arrived with food and guests. Merlin accompanied them. Close behind, Lugh and Fiona materialized followed by Tech Elf and Penelope. "Welcome! A party!" Eliza greeted warmly. After sharing hugs and kisses, they settled down to enjoy Mrs. Claus's delicious meal.

As soon as they finished, they dove into discussing Mittka. Mrs. Claus and Santa filled in Tech Elf and Penelope in on the sequence of recent events including Navva's striking Eliza, which shocked them both. Eliza inserted, "Please do not mention that to anyone and do not think badly of him. Teacher treated him horribly all Navva's life, and he feels intensely disturbed from it. Send him love and light to seek healing."

Very concerned for Navva and Eliza both individually and as a couple, Tech Elf assessed, "Where can he find healing? Certainly not from you, Santa, or Mrs. Claus."

Eliza covered his hand with hers. "You are right. I think Grandfather and Nanna can help, but he must come to that conclusion."

"Have any of you seen him since he hit you, Eliza?" Tech Elf wondered.

All three shook their heads.

"I haven't seen him around the North Pole in the last few days, either. I assume he moved out of Eliza's bedroom," Tech Elf noted.

"When we arrived home the next day, yes, he had taken his belongings and left," Mrs. Claus replied.

"Not surprisingly," Santa added.

Merlin addressed Eliza. "From your description of your interaction with Mittka today, his time frame of need seems to have shortened dramatically. He leaped from forty-eight to twenty-four hours practically overnight."

"Even worse," Eliza expounded, "he kissed more demandingly, longer, and desperately, stealing my breath in the process. He sucked in so much of my air that I didn't know if I could survive the first kiss. I gulped more in quickly and deeply when I had the chance, but I doubted that would be enough to make it through the second kiss. Thankfully, I did. By the third, he seemed to have a sufficient amount to tide him over."

"Until when?" Teeny Tiny Elf blurted, showing his concern.

Merlin assessed, "So not only is the time frame shortening, but his need is escalating."

"Last night we surmised he would be in that state today," Santa disclosed, "and that is why we invited you here tonight. We would like your input in developing a plan to handle this situation and your assistance in implementing the plan."

"How do you relieve Mittka of his addiction?" Fiona wondered.

"We're not certain," Mrs. Claus replied. "Santa, Merlin, and I have ongoing discussions about that."

"We speculate Eliza unknowingly mixes a bit of the red energy she has attached to her from Pan with other energy and channels it," Merlin explained.

"We think she may have begun doing that in response to Mittka's first kisses," Mrs. Claus expanded. Looking at her daughter, she continued, "You had not exhibited this inclination prior to meeting him."

Eliza nodded. "His kisses the first day stimulated me

in a way I have never experienced. Perhaps he unwittingly initiated the process by awakening the red energy I received from Pan."

"Maybe Pan's red energy excited his," Lugh suggested.

"That could be," Santa affirmed.

"He definitely has an attraction to that red energy," Merlin stated. "He doesn't desire Eliza. He craves the energy he pulls from her."

"Which makes the situation particularly dangerous for Eliza," Santa explained. "If Mittka wanted Eliza, she would be able to influence him because he would care about her wishes."

Teeny Tiny Elf interrupted, "But he doesn't. He didn't even notice her bruises today."

Eliza shook her head. "Nor did he mention them."

"So we face two problems," Tech Elf summarized, "a short term one of protecting Eliza and a long term one of weaning Mittka off the red energy he takes from Eliza."

"Exactly," Santa concurred.

"Protection of Eliza is urgent," Merlin cautioned. "Mittka's heightened need is exacting for her. After tomorrow, the excursions are done. How does he get his relief when he is not seeing her regularly?"

"Since his time frame is compacting," Lugh inserted,

"he is forced to set up an easy way to receive gratification anytime."

"The obvious way to accomplish that is to have Eliza handy by taking her," Merlin remarked, "with or without her consent."

Fiona looked at Santa. "What effect does his pulling red energy out of her have on Eliza? That cannot be healthy."

"You are right," Santa agreed. "We have not yet seen a problem, but logic dictates that is it likely."

Malcolm would have been proud to hear his daughter's words. "Eliza must go away." Glancing around the room, Penelope added, "but you have already concluded that, haven't you? That's why Tech Elf and I are here. Our wedding is in a few weeks, and you don't know the long-term solution, when you will devise one, and what executing it will involve."

"That is part of the reason you are here," Santa acknowledged. "We also truly do want your input and help."

As if to dismiss her prior statement, Penelope waved her hand. "I understand that and don't intend to imply you are attempting to break the news to us gently. I wanted to indicate that you have no idea what the long term solution entails and how to implement it."

Collectively, Mrs. Claus, Santa, and Merlin breathed deeply. "You're correct," Merlin stated.

"We are only certain of one thing," Mrs. Claus pronounced. "Eliza is in danger. That danger is rising rapidly, and we must be ready to address it tomorrow."

"Well, okay," Eliza murmured in a soft voice. "Any ideas?"

Everyone sat in silence.

Seemingly out of nowhere Hector, Cory, and Belinda materialized. "We do!" they chorused.

"What?" Eliza asked.

"Kandarry!" Belinda exclaimed. "Contact Kandarry to accompany you on a trip away from here."

"Where?"

"When Patrick and Robin detailed their plan," Lugh remembered, "they described the interviews as part one."

Eliza picked up his thought. "That's right! They planned to give their input for part two and introduce me to other devas in part three. Could they conduct parts two and three someplace other than here?"

"Let's ask them," Santa suggested, telepathically requesting Patrick and Robin to join them immediately.

They arrived in seconds. Santa reviewed the situation, the discussion, and the suggestion. "What do you think?"

"We realized that Mittka has a problem," Patrick replied. "That's why we have made attempts to interrupt him, as you have noticed."

"We apologize, Eliza, for what you are going through," Robin added. "We never envisioned Mittka's presence would cause this upset."

"How would you know?" Eliza soothed. "How could any of us have known?"

"We're still not certain what is going on," Merlin acknowledged.

"Or what to do about it," Teeny Tiny Elf finished.

Patrick shared a look with Robin. "We could easily complete the rest of the interviews for the tree deva book away from here."

"After tomorrow's interview, doing so might be better for all concerned," Robin concurred.

"Okay," Santa responded. "We appreciate your help. When you arrive in the morning, act normally. Do not give any indication of a change." Santa paused, thinking. "I think we might be smart to have Patrick and Robin appear to be leaving as per usual but have them accompany us to the North Pole." He looked at Mrs. Claus and then Merlin. "What do you think?"

"In order to have them take Eliza and Kandarry to their first stop?" Merlin surmised.

"Not the first interview," Mrs. Claus urged, "but a place they think would be safe until the interview."

"Have you given Mittka a clue of which devas you had planned to approach for the upcoming interviews?" Santa wondered.

Patrick and Robin looked at each other. Hesitantly, Robin replied, "I don't think so."

"He's so caught up in red energy that he hasn't asked, either," Patrick added, "which is unlike him."

"Choose a safe one to start," Santa requested. "If you have any inkling Mittka might guess your choices, please change them. We'll leave that in your hands."

"We will," Patrick affirmed. "Anything else?"

"Keep in contact with us about when you will be meeting, where, and with whom," Santa added. "I want to cloak all meetings in a way Mittka cannot detect."

"We'll discuss this further when we leave here," Robin assured everyone. "We want to keep Eliza safe."

"See you in the morning. We will plan to go home with you tomorrow," Patrick offered as they vanished.

As if on cue that she was next, Kandarry appeared. Having read Santa's next move in his mind, Eliza had invited her over immediately. Knowing her best friend would readily agree, Eliza asked, "Would you take a trip with me?"

"Sure. Where?"

"We don't know yet," Eliza replied. "I'll fill you in later."

"We want Eliza to get away from danger," Mrs. Claus noted. "Go home, tell your parents you are going away with Eliza, and inform them I will stop by tomorrow afternoon with details. Meet in our kitchen at the North Pole shortly before noon tomorrow."

"Do **not** come here," Santa emphasized.

"See you there," Kandarry remarked as she left for home.

"Tomorrow I want to remove anyone Mittka could use to force me to accompany him," Eliza mused. "Dusty and Chance, Teeny Tiny Elf..."

"I'm coming with you!" he announced.

Everyone became silent, thinking. Would that be smart? Would Teeny Tiny Elf be an impediment? Perhaps he could be helpful. No one could come up with a reason to keep him home.

Santa voiced their conclusions. "I guess that's alright." He locked his gaze with Teeny Tiny Elf's. "You have an uncanny knack of alerting Eliza to danger. Be careful. If either one of you thinks the situation is unsafe for Teeny Tiny Elf, come home, okay?"

Teeny Tiny Elf could not fudge his answer to Santa. "Okay."

"What about Dusty and Chance?" Eliza asked anxiously. "Mittka might threaten or worse take them to make me comply."

"When we return tomorrow, Mrs. Claus and I will go home. Patrick and Robin will tag along with us–"

"I am not staying in the house this time," Eliza emphatically pronounced. "I am too confined here to deal with Mittka."

"You're right," Santa agreed. "However you will arrive back in the house with us and need to give Mittka the opportunity to leave as per usual so that he can return. If the dogs go home with us at that point, Mittka's suspicions will be aroused. We will probably transport later than him. Once we are gone, go outside along with Teeny Tiny Elf. Have Dusty and Chance stay in the house so that Mittka encounters them when he comes back."

"Be very aware of acting normally," Merlin advised. "Taking you with him will be critical for Mittka, and he will likely be on the alert for anything that may get in his way."

"When do I transport them?" Eliza asked, urgency in her voice.

"Once you see Mittka approaching you, transport them," Santa responded.

"Okay." She turned to Lugh and Fiona. "Stay inside. I'm certain I will shoot bolts at Mittka. I don't want stray ones to hurt you."

"Have you ever shot a stray bolt?" Lugh scoffed.

"No, but just thinking about this makes me nervous. I'm not sure what my nervous tension might trigger."

"In the past nerves have prompted you to be even more accurate, if that's possible," Santa noted. He paused. "I echo Eliza's suggestion for different reasons. Don't give Mittka a target to grab. You might want to go to work with Fiona tomorrow, Lugh."

With a long, concerned look at Eliza, Lugh reluctantly agreed. "Yeah, that's a good idea. I will. I'm sure Fiona can find something for me to do."

She sighed. "I'll get more done just knowing you are not in the middle of the fray. Sorry, Eliza."

Eliza smiled. "I do not want him there, either." She paused, considering all aspects. "When does Teeny Tiny Elf transport?"

Santa hesitated. "You two determine that based on what's happening."

Eliza turned to Teeny Tiny Elf. In an unusually stern

voice, she ordered, "Once you transport, do not come back to check on me. Mittka will instantly recognize that controlling you is a very easy way to make me compliant. Stay in Mother's kitchen and wait."

Teeny Tiny Elf stared at Eliza. "I don't know if I can do that." He sighed. "But I'll try."

Eliza addressed her dad. "When do you enter the picture?"

"If he isn't scared off by your bolts, which, sadly, I don't expect him to be," Santa explained, "you will resort to a freeze. Once you freeze him, contact me, and I'll be right there." He drew a deep breath. "I have no idea how long even your strongest freeze will hold him. I will transport him as far away as I can before he shakes it off. You transport out as fast as you can. When he gets rid of your freeze, he will come right back for you."

"His drive for your red energy will be so great that taking you will be his only option," Merlin stressed. "He'll do that with or without your cooperation. While Mittka has been very friendly, which is his usual nature, he currently is not his usual self. Realize that elementals consider him a god for a reason. He has strong powers."

"Stronger than you and Dad?"

"We don't know, and we don't want to test him," Merlin cautioned.

"Your father and Merlin," Mrs. Claus noted, "have always had the attitude that they are not in a contest to decide who has the greater power."

Eliza nodded. "I understand. I don't want to know, either."

Santa addressed Tech Elf and Penelope, "If we can figure out what to do to help Mittka, we may need to use Eliza and your wedding to lure him to her."

For the first time that evening, Penelope smiled. "Will you be back for our wedding?"

"Yes," Eliza definitively stated. "I would not miss it."

Penelope locked eyes with Tech Elf. "If that will help Eliza...and Mittka," she offered without hesitation, "we're fine with it."

"We are and look forward to seeing you there," Tech Elf agreed.

"Your mother and I want you to contact us every day so that we know you are safe," Santa directed. "I am applying an extremely sensitive tracer on you which will let me know if Mittka is nearby. I echo Merlin's caution. Mittka is very powerful. This red energy has caused him to go out of control. An out-of-control powerful being is particularly dangerous, especially toward the being to whom he has become addicted. This situation is very serious."

Eliza nodded. "I understand, Dad."

"Me, too," Teeny Tiny Elf echoed.

Before leaving, everyone shared a tight hug and kiss with Eliza, sending her enormous doses of love and light. Her parents left last. "See you in the morning," Mrs. Claus whispered.

"Yes, see you in the morning," Santa repeated.

The four parted with knots in their solar plexuses.

Chapter 26

Eliza awakened the next morning feeling apprehensive. Continuing to lie in bed for a while, she directed her thoughts toward the day. She managed to calm her churning nerves and mind by forcing herself to meditate. Teeny Tiny Elf remained blissfully unaware that she was awake. He'll need this rest, she advised herself. Let him be.

Detecting she was alert, Hector, Cory, and Belinda appeared at her feet. "We are thankful you are going away," Belinda whispered.

"While we never dreamed of saying that, we think right now it's the best move," Cory added softly, trying not to wake Teeny Tiny Elf.

"We're very worried about you," Hector finished.

She had not considered Mittka might be a danger to them, but the thought suddenly struck her. "Will you guys be okay? Can you hide from Mittka? I want you to be safe."

They nodded in unison. "Don't worry. We have already considered that possibility," Cory replied.

"We have each identified dark spaces in the house we can blend into," Hector informed.

"Focus on Mittka, the dogs, and Teeny Tiny Elf," Belinda recommended. "We will take care of ourselves."

Eliza spread her arms wide. "Give me a group hug."

As she sat up, they hopped into her lap. She gave them each a kiss on the cheek. "I love you three and will miss you. Please, please take care of yourselves. He might come back."

"I doubt he will be able to gain entry," Belinda conjectured.

"Why?" Eliza wondered.

"We think Santa will seal up the house, blocking Mittka access," Hector returned.

Eliza was shocked. "Will that affect you?"

"Not a bit," Cory offered.

She gently hugged them one more time. With a tear

trickling down her cheek, she bid them good-bye, released them, and slid out of bed. Tip-toeing to the bathroom, Eliza showered, dressed, and exited just as Teeny Tiny Elf woke up. Stepping over to him, she kissed him on the cheek. "Good morning!"

"Morning," he mumbled.

"I'm headed to the kitchen to make breakfast. When you are ready, join me."

A few minutes later, Teeny Tiny Elf dragged himself to a chair in the kitchen. "Are you okay?" Eliza wondered.

He started to reply, choked up, and stopped. Eliza picked him up and hugged him. "What's wrong?"

He clung to her. "I'm scared," he whispered. "I'm scared you won't make it through your fight with Mittka."

She smiled. "You weren't scared when we stood up to the powers of greed."

"I had confidence in you," he asserted, "and you didn't give me time to think about it. I hardly slept last night, seeing Mittka's face with his crazy, obsessed look. That scares me." He paused. "He might be more powerful than Santa and Merlin. Do you think you can handle him?"

"I'm not afraid. I'm at a point that I'd rather confront him than continue to cope with his insistent kisses." She mirrored his pause. "Do I have a choice?"

He pulled away, smiling into her eyes and touching her lips with his finger. "I was so sorry to see how his mean kisses hurt your lips."

"Today we will do something about that." She brightened. "I am glad you are coming along with Kandarry and me. We will have a fun time!"

She set him back down in the chair. Cheered by her upbeat mood, Teeny Tiny Elf devoured breakfast hungrily. They cleaned up and waited for Santa and Mrs. Claus, who arrived shortly. Their tight hugs and kisses that lingered a bit too long felt more like good-bye than good morning. Before they exchanged a word, Patrick and Robin appeared followed by Mittka.

"Good morning," Eliza greeted. "Where are we visiting today?"

"Good morning," Patrick and Robin chorused.

"We are visiting an ancient forest," Robin replied.

Although he didn't say a word, Mittka's unwavering stare at Eliza's lips spoke volumes. *I don't want to be stuck seeing his obsessive look every day,* she thought, strengthening her resolve to be away from him.

"Ready, Santa," Patrick nudged.

Santa immediately transported them into the midst of tall redwood trees. "Where are we?" Eliza wondered, speaking in a hushed tone.

"Muir Woods," Robin answered.

"Near San Francisco? I've heard of them but never visited," Eliza remarked.

Tipping her head back, she gazed up, struggling to see the tree tops. "Likely you will not see them," Patrick noted.

"You're right," she confirmed. Glancing around, she asked, "Which trees are speaking with us?"

"I am," replied a tree directly in front of her.

Eliza bowed. "I am privileged to meet you."

Robin introduced, "Yes, thank you for granting us an interview. Eliza, who is writing the book, is in front of you. By her side are her parents, Santa and Mrs. Claus, and their special family member Teeny Tiny Elf. Next to Patrick is Mittka."

"All of us are pleased to have you visit. Welcome, Mittka. Santa and Mrs. Claus, we have heard a great deal about you and are honored to have you who do so much for the Earth grace our forest with your presence," the tree returned.

"Thank you. What an extraordinary place!" Mrs. Claus remarked. "Only one other time have I experienced the pervasive calm and peaceful atmosphere you create here."

"I was thinking just those words," Eliza concurred. "I am awed by the trees' magnificence and blown away by their environment."

Eliza was shocked by the tree asking her a question. "Patrick and Robin tell me this is your eighth interview. In them, what has surprised you the most?"

She paused, thinking. "I thought fungi hurt trees. I now understand the network of fungi work in cooperation with trees, helping them in many ways."

"Whenever any being is not in good health, that being is susceptible to illness. Fungi can inadvertently introduce microbes that are harmful to trees in a weakened condition. If the tree is in ill health, it is vulnerable, giving the microbes an opportunity. Recently someone dear to you exhibited behavior resulting from an unhealthy frame of mind. That being's mental health opened the door to his actions, not the situation."

Immediately grasping the tree's reference to Navva and possibly Mittka, Eliza agreed. "I understand you. Thank you for clarifying that for me." She added, "My neighbor delights in stating he likes a 'clean woods.' Would you comment on that?"

"I believe humans' attitude toward cleanliness and trees' environment do not jive. Natural conditions tend to be messy, at least to humans. Tidy natural habitats do not exist, due mostly to so many creatures working to survive and contributing to the surroundings in their own unique ways," the tree explained. "What humans view as unclean we enjoy as the normal process of life."

"I feel that cleaning up woods takes away important elements necessary for life," Eliza noted.

"That is true."

"Some human experts today state that we can learn a great deal from ancient forests. Do you agree?"

Eliza received the impression of a chuckle from the tree. "Yes and no. Time contributes to an environment. Citing characteristics of past beings and thinking they can help with today's challenges may not be helpful, depending upon how the information is used. The answer to current problems does not lie in recreating the past because the effect of time is not taken into consideration—"

"Wait! Are you saying that time itself has an impact on the environment?" Eliza wondered.

"Yes. Humans do not understand time. Their lack of understanding greatly affects how they interpret and perceive past environs because they ignore time's role."

"So trying to recreate a past habitat and leaving out time will not work?" Eliza questioned.

"Right. Rather than comparing the current situation with a past one, humans would be smart to assess what they see today. Using that information will incorporate time's effect now without a necessity to understand time."

Eliza's mind whirled. "Wow! I must mull that over." She shifted the subject. "Let's move to age. You have been around hundreds of years, a difficult number for humans to comprehend. What is your advice to humans on age?"

"Many humans today do not revere age. Every stage of life offers an opportunity. The older stage may contain wisdom garnered from a lifetime of experiences. I have greater insight today than hundreds of years ago. Patrick and Robin are wisely tapping into that. Humans would be smart to do the same with their seniors," the tree advised.

"Why is your bark red?" Eliza wondered.

"The tannic acid in my bark and heartwood has a reddish tone."

"Tannic acid? Is that what gives you resistance to fire?" Eliza queried.

"Yes. In addition to being resistant, if my bark is burned, I can re-sprout from the burnt tissue."

Awed, Eliza continued, "I want to ask more about color. Your beautiful red strikes me as more of a rose pink which has the characteristics of selflessness and gentleness. Does that resonate with you?"

"It does. Interesting that you mention red. Woods all over the planet have a great deal of interaction with red," the tree revealed.

"Really?! How?"

"Hunters roam woods. Even though their main objective is spilling red blood via the hunt, an equally important goal is seeking the assistance of trees."

"What help can trees give hunters?" Eliza questioned.

"As you know red is the color of anger, irritability, present-centeredness, excitement, and a physical approach, to name a few. Exposure to red in large doses can cause overstimulation. More than any other group, hunters have red around them in varying degrees. Green, the color of forests, is balancing. Green renews, helps control the heart, and offers peacefulness and security. Green is a good antidote for red. Without consciously acknowledging their need, hunters seek the green of forests to alleviate the red around them," the tree explained.

"I have never heard that association before," Mrs. Claus blurted. "Thank you. That is fascinating!"

"I agree," Eliza added. "I have one more request. You've lived hundreds of years. What single piece of advice do you have for humans?"

"Slow down. Take time to walk among the trees, advice Patrick shared you received from trees in your last interview. Learn to meditate. That would help with challenges facing humans, trees, and the planet right now."

The tree had provided such an informative interview that Eliza had forgotten what faced her shortly. Caught up in the tree's wisdom, Eliza knelt and touched one of the tree's roots. "Thank you. I am truly honored to be in your presence, to have spoken with you, and to communicate your thoughts to others."

Teeny Tiny Elf joined Eliza. "Yes, thank you, magnificent tree. I am grateful to have met you, too."

Mrs. Claus and Santa echoed that sentiment. Mittka remained silent, desperately struggling to maintain his composure until he could kiss Eliza. Patrick and Robin profusely thanked the tree and the entire woods.

The redwood directed one last statement to Eliza before they transported back to her kitchen. "We send along with you an enormous dose of light and love as you continue on your journey."

Smiling, she mouthed "Thank you" as the group disappeared.

They had barely materialized when Mittka waved and vanished, grappling with his addiction. Without a good-bye, hug, or kiss, Santa, Mrs. Claus, Patrick, and Robin also left. Eliza picked up Teeny Tiny Elf, slid open the sunroom door, and raced to the Little Tree. She knew Mittka would appear in her office any second.

He did. He waited a couple minutes and realized that he didn't hear any sounds in the house. Stepping out of the office, he called, "Eliza? Eliza, where are you?"

Looking up and down the hall, he didn't see any movement. Hesitantly, he walked to the kitchen. No one there, either. Out of the corner of his eye, he caught a motion outside. Quickly moving through the living room, he glanced out the window at the Little Tree. Eliza and Teeny Tiny Elf stood beside it, touching its branches.

Curious as to what had drawn them outside, Mittka followed.

"We only have a few seconds to say good-bye," Eliza whispered. "I'm about to have an altercation with Mittka. Then I'm going away for a while. I love you, Little Tree. I'm adding nine layers of impenetrable protection to you. That's the only way I can shield you. I hope it's enough." Teary-eyed, she kissed one branch and brushed several others.

"I love you, too," the Little Tree returned. "Watch out. I see him coming around the corner by the deck."

"Let's get away from the Little Tree," Eliza suggested, grabbing Teeny Tiny Elf's hand. They began to stroll down the path toward the woods. "Remember," she whispered. "When I shoot my first bolt, you transport."

"What about the dogs?" Teeny Tiny Elf asked anxiously.

"Barney took them out in the yard just before we got back. I'm transporting them now."

"Eliza!" Mittka hollered. "Eliza! Where are you going?"

She turned and halted. "Don't come closer, Mittka. I'm not giving you any more kisses."

Nothing she could have said would have had greater shock value. "What?! What did you say?"

"Stop! Do not come any closer." For clarity, she repeated, "I'm not giving you kisses any more. You have an addiction, Mittka, that you need to fix. I am no longer satisfying your addiction."

He continued his approach, thinking to pull her into his arms and erase her speech. Simultaneously, she dropped Teeny Tiny Elf's hand and shot a bolt on Mittka's right side. As Teeny Tiny Elf disappeared, Eliza shot a bolt on Mittka's left side. "I said, 'Stop!'"

Not expecting her bolts, Mittka jumped back. "You didn't tell me you could shoot bolts!"

"You never asked."

Raising his foot to step forward, Eliza shot another bolt on his left side.

"So that's the way you want to play it, huh?!" he spouted ominously. "Do you think you are powerful enough to handle me?"

She didn't reply.

He shot a strong bolt at her. Her bolt countered and sent it back at him. He couldn't return it to her and dodged it, veering right.

In quick succession, he shot two bolts at Eliza. She boomeranged both back to him.

"Those were a couple of lucky returns," Mittka yelled. "You can't outlast me. I am more powerful than you ever dreamed of being."

Standing her ground, Eliza calmly waited for his next shots. Wanting to keep her intact so that he could get her kisses, he offered, "C'mon. End this foolishness. Give me a kiss."

Eliza remained silent.

"Okay," Mittka placated. "I'll send three more to make you feel powerful. If you return them, come over and give me a kiss. We'll say that you won." He paused. "If you don't give me a kiss then, we're in a shoot out."

Eliza exhibited the calm of Santa and Mrs. Claus. Had Mittka not been so distressed, he might have noticed. He didn't.

His three rapid-fire shots did not phase Eliza. She had easily countered more during the fight with the powers of greed. They flashed back to him faster than he anticipated.

After a three-step dodge-dance of his bolts coming back at him, Mittka stopped, smiled, and motioned for her to come to him.

She didn't budge.

Their back-and-forth had sapped the little bit of civility he had left. Changing to a sinister stance, he sneered, "Sorry. It's been nice knowing you."

He sent nine bolts at Eliza, one almost on top of the next. She returned them all just as fast. He doubled the number and shot eighteen. Again, she boomeranged them back to him. Thinking to catch her off guard, he shot six, increased his speed with nine more, and significantly slowed with a final six. She returned all at the speed he had used.

Her competency ignited his rage. He wouldn't be beaten, especially by a woman!

Certain Eliza couldn't continue to keep up with him, he shot thirty, then sixty, and finally ninety, all in the fastest succession he had ever used. She returned all. When the ninetieth one reached Mittka, he had run down on energy to dodge. His foot slid, and he fell.

Mittka lying on the ground gave Eliza the opportunity she sought. She instantly sent the strongest freeze she could muster at him, causing him to be unconscious but not feel the cold. Simultaneously, she telepathically reached Santa, *Ready.*

Santa instantly appeared. She smiled and took off for the house to grab her bag and transport to the North Pole.

Pulling her bag from under the bed, Eliza hurried back to the kitchen for transport. She returned at the same time as Navva materialized. They both halted in shock. "Eliza," Navva croaked. "Eliza…"

"Get out of here!" she commanded. "Get out! Get out!"

Knowing she didn't have time for an explanation, she transported, hoping that he would listen and follow her lead.

The house was silent. Navva called the dogs and roamed through each room, searching for a friend. No one. He glanced out the living room window at the Little Tree where he had seen Eliza kissing Mittka. Transporting out to the Little Tree, he murmured, "Little Tree, how are you?"

The Little Tree echoed Eliza's tone and words. "Navva! Get out! Get out! Get out…Now! Go back to the North Pole. You are in grave danger!"

Feeling an outcast, Navva hung his head. No one wanted him around. Despondent and unloved, he left, transporting back to the North and South Pacific Dome where he had been sitting on the beach. His father's words had sunk in. On impulse Navva had decided to apologize to Eliza and make amends. Her strongly ordering him away had crushed his fragile confidence. He felt more lost than ever.

Navva had barely left when Mittka appeared, red with rage. He didn't know how he had gotten where he woke up, but he was furious. Transporting into the house, he searched everywhere for Eliza, the dogs, and Teeny Tiny Elf. As he did, Hector, Cory, and Belinda shifted their hiding places so that he wouldn't detect them.

Outside, the Little Tree telepathically contacted Santa. *Navva came and went. Mittka's back. Is Navva at the North Pole?*

Before he received Santa's reply, Mittka rushed out of the house. Shaking with anger, he cursed Eliza. "I'll wipe out the place and tree you love so much!"

Sending a strong blast at the house, garage, and Little Tree, Mittka disappeared so as not to be caught up in the explosion.

When Eliza appeared in her mother's kitchen, everyone

there breathed a deep sigh of relief. Santa's disappearance in response to her telepathic message had assured them she had managed to freeze Mittka, but they had more to do.

"You made it!" Teeny Tiny Elf screamed, leaping into her arms.

Dusty and Chance ran over to her, wagging their tails.

They did not have time for a celebration. "Navva appeared just as I was about to transport," Eliza related to her mother. "Would you ask Rory if he has seen Navva?"

"I will," Mrs. Claus anxiously replied. "We'll take care of it. You must go—"

With a quick good-bye kiss to her mother, Dusty, and Chance, Eliza and Teeny Tiny Elf moved beside Patrick, Robin, and Kandarry, and they disappeared.

Get the sixth Eliza book
The Healing Touch

Santa is misreading Eliza's mind. How can that happen? Meanwhile, he is instructing her on freezing and shooting lightning bolts. Grandfather is teaching her healing. At his lessons she meets and becomes acquainted with Navva, who has a troubled upbringing. The story builds to a terrifying climax.

Available now!

Get the fifth Eliza book
Riding the Rainbow

Eliza was attacked in her sleep. Kandarry came to Eliza's rescue, but something was not right with either one of them. How can they be fixed? While Santa and Merlin try to figure that out, Eliza launches into the third part of the prophecy, learning about fairies and color. They are a lot of fun! Eliza finally tours Mrs. Claus's Growing Grounds, which are amazing! However, the threat to Eliza and Kandarry is relentless. Who is after them? Can they be stopped?

Available now!

Get the fourth Eliza book
Teeny Tiny Elf's Mistake

Teeny Tiny Elf's Mistake caused grave upset in the North Pole Family. As Estel and Oakley reveal previously undisclosed information about elves to Eliza through six excursions, an event threatens to make Eliza disappear forever, and wizards don't know how to handle it. An elemental group's members who are ignored clamor for attention. What will be the outcome of these three situations?

Available now!

Get the third Eliza book
The Trapped Wizard

When Eliza decided to focus on trolls as the first elemental group to feature in her books, she had no idea what she was about to encounter. In the process of meeting trolls and learning through them, she developed a deep respect and affection for those individuals. She also stumbled across a slimy character with a scheme that was dangerous to trolls and humans. Find out the obstacles she confronts, the challenges she faces, and the solutions she helps implement.

Available now!

Get the second Eliza book

The Last Christmas Tree

Did you know Santa rescues hundreds of Christmas trees left on the lot Christmas Eve because they hadn't found a home? When Santa and Teeny Tiny Elf picked up the last Christmas tree of the season, they unintentionally set in motion events that would change their lives forever. As the events unfolded, mysteries were solved, danger threatened from an unknown source, and unexpected occurrences tipped their world upside down.

Available now!

Get the first Eliza book

Trouble at the North Pole

Alex Malone had had enough. He was tired of maintaining that Santa existed when he could never see him. He decided to prove that Santa didn't exist, initiating a media campaign and a sponsored contest challenging children to "catch" Santa Christmas Eve. Santa found out and asked Eliza to help him handle the situation. Her suggestions led Santa, Teeny Tiny Elf, and everyone at the North Pole on an adventure they will always remember – and so will Alex.

Available now!

A Note from the Author

Similar to books five, six, and seven, books eight, nine, and ten are another trilogy within the Eliza series with one difference. I am not releasing all three at once. I apologize for that and warn you that book nine will leave you hanging. I am in the process of writing book ten and plan to release it next year. The first trilogy surprised me. To have that followed immediately by a second zoomed me to a new level of amazement.

When I began writing *The Disturbance*, the opening scene kept going on and on. I wondered when it would end. So much happens in a riveting fashion. During the entire book, I continued to be stunned at the revelations. I suspect you will feel the same. The storyline spilled over into book nine, *Mittka*, with Eliza still gathering information on leprechauns and pursuing the fourth prophecy. She begins to learn about tree devas, which she will finalize in book ten.

I am grateful to you for sharing Eliza's journey with me. I hope you continue to come along on her future adventures.

Elizabeth

Listen to the audio read by the author

of all the Eliza books at monarchtreepublishing.com

I have personally recorded in audio books one through seven. Doing the recording in my voice gives you, the listener, the story in my inflections, which inserts additional richness and insight into the telling. You may rent the audio of each book for a two-week time period. Go to monarchtreepublishing.com to do that. Enjoy!

Elizabeth

PS I will have books eight and nine recorded soon.